The Five-Year Guide to Self-Sufficiency

Amelia Barrows

DEDICATION

To my mother, who raised me in a garden and ensured that fast-food restaurants were always a place of mystery and vague temptation. You let me wander through the desert with skinned knees and nothing but my horse, dogs, and imagination when other girls were handed dolls. Best of all, you forgave me when I decided I'd rather raise chickens and goats than spend the rest of my life in a cubicle. The older I get, the more I value the upbringing you gave me.

CONTENTS

INTRODUCTION

THE MODERN SELF-SUFFICIENCY MOVEMENT

Our ancestors spent hundreds of thousands of years living in a world of hunger and danger, faced with the constant prospect of starvation. Life was short, hard, and uncomfortable; on the timeline of evolution, homes and agriculture are recent luxuries. The only reality we knew could be shaped with our own two hands, and, unlike any animal before us, we shaped. We built, we invented, and we expanded to dominate every inhabitable space on Earth. We raised ourselves out of the dust and into prosperity.

As a consequence, humanity has changed. Life is now divided into the physical and the digital, and the lines between them are further blurred every day. We are creatures of the abstract, quick to adapt and eager to move forward, but all too willing to forget the experiences of those who came before us.

The current generation of young adults grew up with the Internet. They spend an average of eight hours a day in front of a screen,[1] and they feel uncomfortable without a gadget in their hands. They were raised in an environment that values and facilitates the sharing of skills. They create, design, write, and work together, but they have no idea how to take care of themselves. And it's not just the kids.

The majority of Americans are not stupid, lazy, or helpless, but there's no denying that we now delegate nearly all aspects of our own survival to others and are woefully ignorant of our food supply. Fruits and vegetables are flawless and uniform through the liberal application of pesticides, herbicides, and genetic modification. Meat is vacuum-packed and far removed from the animals slaughtered to produce it. Bacon doesn't come from a pig anymore; it comes from the grocery store.

This detachedness can be traced back to the 1950s, when America's newly-cemented position as a global superpower led to a culture that thrived on rampant consumerism. Corporations grew, and advertising with them, pushing the ideal of a family that could afford to buy instead of make. Manual labor was seen as a symptom of poverty and lower class. Americans entered a decades-long love affair with letting anonymous, minimum-wage workers take care of the petty details of life.

Such a lifestyle can only continue for so long, however. Right now, the developed world is at a crossroad. Despite increasing regulations, the food industry is constantly finding ways to cheapen its products, even at the cost of human health. High-fructose corn syrup, soy, and preservatives are everywhere. Sugar, once a rare treat, now lurks in the most unexpected places to satiate palates accustomed to sweetness. Our pork and chicken are injected with saline solution to add weight and flavor.

Crops lining the roads of rural America are now labeled by their GMO strains. The companies that manufacture these seeds promote herbicide-resistance in weeds and sue farmers for the natural spread of their own crops. Government subsidies and economies of scale favor huge corporations that decimate small farms as well as the environment. For every calorie of food produced in the United States, farms expend ten more in fossil fuels.[2]

Meanwhile, rising gas prices and widespread drought are driving up the prices of these composite foods to record levels. We are paying more for meals that have been molded and processed to contain as little food as possible.

No matter how much corporations like to pretend otherwise, these practices are not sustainable. Massive industrialized agriculture is going to hit a wall, and when it does the consequences may be swift and brutal. The United States has not had to deal with widespread food shortages since the Civil War. Today, when a storm disrupts the supply line to grocery stores, food runs out in days. The vast majority of Americans are not prepared to go a week without access to easy and plentiful food and water shipped from thousands of miles away.

The problem with this situation is that no matter how many red flags pop up, altering this trajectory is nearly impossible. Now that power has been consolidated within a few companies, there is simply too much money to be lost in a structural revolution. They are much closer to your elected representatives than you could ever hope to be, and they have a lot more to offer. At this point, the only way to lessen the damage of an impending crash is to extricate yourself from the system as entirely as possible. This is the base ideology behind most members of the self-sufficiency movement.

Whether you are preparing for catastrophe or simply want to practice a healthier and more independent lifestyle, taking control of your own resources is an enlightening, if challenging, experience. Establishing a small farm requires backbreaking labor and long hours in all weather. And yet, despite this, the search for a better quality of life has drawn individuals from all different backgrounds.

Learning to go without the constant fixation on class, status, and displays of wealth our society values so highly is the first step toward a new perspective: one that recognizes the difference between hollow happiness and fulfillment. You can enjoy modern conveniences without having to buy into a modern culture that demands a new car and smart phone every year.

How you go about transforming your life, and to what extent, is up to you. Any change for the better is well worth the effort. Unfortunately, many people quit before they even begin. When faced with the prospect of empty acres and a long to-do list, it is easy to stall and never regain your momentum.

This book is meant to serve as a rough guide through the transition period, offering advice on where to start and how to progress year by year in a logical and manageable way.

THE SELF-SUFFICIENT MINDSET

Having been raised in a culture of self-sufficiency and taught to embrace every aspect of nature, I sometimes forget that not everyone is so enamored with the realities of life on a homestead. After all, the children of farmers began their mass exodus to the cities for a reason.

For every idyllic moment spent picking tomatoes in the garden, there is another spent cutting an animal's throat or chopping firewood while knee-deep in snow. You will go to bed exhausted and aching, and at some point you will injure yourself. Money will be tight, even when you trim the fat you have been trained for decades to think of as "necessary." Vacations become a thing of the past, because there is simply too much depending on your care to leave. The truth is that homesteading is difficult, dirty, and demanding.

I am not saying this to frighten you off, but it *is* a warning. It takes an odd sort of individual to seek out so much trouble when everything is already available at the nearest box store. If you are not willing to make fundamental changes to the way you live, you are better off starting a small garden and supporting your local co-op or farmer's market.

Teamwork, even within a basic family unit, is critical on a farm. The division of labor once seen in rural families arose because there is simply too much for any one person to do. You don't have to divide everything along traditional gender roles, but accomplishing everything in this book is only possible with help.

The big question going into a project like this is: How much is enough? Do you want fresh vegetables in the summer, or do you want to go completely off the grid on a rural mountainside? It is a personal question, and only you can know when your quest for self-sufficiency is at an end.

Until then, stick with it. The early days are the hardest, when everything still needs to be settled and learned and cultivated, but the decades that follow reap equal rewards over and over again.

IS TRUE SELF-SUFFICIENCY POSSIBLE?

Solitary animals like the tiger and weasel are self-sufficient for most of their lives. Humans are not. We are hardwired to live together and benefit from mutual cooperation. Those who cut themselves off from society miss a vital part of human nature and struggle when an inevitable catastrophe occurs.

Truly self-sufficient homesteads raise sheep and sew their own clothes, grow their own grains and forage, recycle sewage, don't own a car, and don't need to barter or spend money to survive. They live in remote areas where legal authorities won't reinforce housing regulations. It is an extreme lifestyle that very few people wish for.

I do not advocate striving for complete self-sufficiency. Instead, in this guide, I have diluted the phrase to mean the ability to supply all of a family's needs, rather than everything a household consumes.

Most homesteaders still buy clothing from department stores, browse the internet, and watch television. They balance these external influences with a strong relationship to the earth and a detailed appreciation of how it sustains them.

The basic ingredients of life for every human being can be divided into four categories: water, food, housing, and energy.

Water

Without water, nothing else matters. A healthy person can last a little over a week without access to it, but contaminated water kills just as quickly as dehydration. Having enough clean water for your family is not enough. Livestock also need it to survive, as do plants. It isn't as inspiring or rewarding as the sight of a garden overflowing with produce, but collecting and purifying water should be a top priority for anyone with disaster scenarios in mind. Everything else can be hunted, grown, or improvised, but water is the inescapable barrier to life that cannot be ignored.

Food

Like water, food is a nonnegotiable part of human survival. Our bodies must take in energy to expend it both in active movement and to generate heat, breathe, and digest food. We also require minerals and vitamins to complete the chemical processes that drive our complex systems.

Some foods are more energy-efficient than others. The food chain is a pyramid, with solar energy fueling the bottom and apex predators at the top. The sun's rays feed plants, which collect a small fraction of that energy and are in turn eaten by an herbivore. If that herbivore is consumed by a predator, the predator gains less energy than the herbivore did from the plants. It's why farmers raise rabbits and chickens instead of foxes.

Find the right balance between resource intensity and your own tastes while establishing a homestead. A family of four burns through approximately 10,000 calories a day- more if everyone is doing hard physical labor. That number is easier and cheaper to reach growing only grains, fruits, and vegetables, but most families believe that meat is worth the added effort.

Housing

People can live without shelter, but it isn't pleasant. Exposure to the elements in colder climates leads to frostbite and eventually death, and life under a blazing sun isn't much better. For this reason, every practical farm has a place for humans and livestock alike to get away from the weather and predatory animals.

The ideal farmhouse is just large enough to hold a family. It should be well-ventilated in summer but insulated enough to protect against the chill of winter. Most families getting into self-sufficiency already have a house to work with, but others prefer to buy a large tract of empty land and build from there. While house construction is not covered in this book, it can be much less expensive than retrofitting a home for energy efficiency.

Energy

Most people enjoy the perks of electricity. It powers lights, air conditioning, computers, freezers, and even well pumps. Self-sufficiency does not mandate becoming a Luddite; taking advantage of modern technology is common sense. At the same time, anyone who has gone through a power outage knows how fragile electricity really is. A few downed lines can leave millions without power for weeks. Standard or alternative energy is part of almost every modern homestead, but a self-sufficient individual also possesses the tools and knowledge to perform critical tasks without the assistance of electricity.

Each of these four basic needs take time and money to develop on a farm. Depending on your commitment and resources, you may be able to achieve rudimentary self-sufficiency within a single year.

A year-long timeframe to accomplish so much, however, is usually not feasible. This book takes that fact into consideration and instead charts out a slow progression over the course of five years. Each year builds upon the last, allowing your farm to progress naturally and with as little financial strain as possible. It's not an encyclopedia, which can overwhelm beginners, nor is it an in-depth examination of any of the topics covered. It is, rather, a map to set you on the right path with the necessary information to begin a sustainable lifestyle.

LAND

The amount of land required to achieve self-sufficiency is the subject of much debate and personal opinion. A single person can eke out a living on two acres and make a respectable showing on just one. With careful planning, some apartment-dwellers grow dozens or hundreds of pounds of produce on roofs and balconies. Other families grow all of their fruits and vegetables on half an acre through tight spacing and intensive management.

Realistically, though, buy as much quality land as you can afford. Approximately 25 acres is a good number, and 40 is better, but even five acres will do. Land is one of the soundest investments you can make, so grab as much as you can to avoid regretting it later.

The 25 acre figure I personally throw around is based on the assumption that the land in question is well hydrated and fertile. Scrubland or extremely rocky soil is usually more trouble than it is worth but, on the other hand, developed farmland is quite expensive. Wooded lands and meadows with a nearby water source are often the best mix of quality and price.

If you want to provide your own heat, plan to have five acres or more of forest. A stream or river on the property is also a major asset. Every natural resource your land lacks must be supplied in some other way.

When applicable, this guide discusses how much space is necessary for a certain type of livestock or plant, as well as how many it takes to feed a single adult. Although I recognize the possibility of self-sufficiency without significant acreage, this book does assume that the reader has at least five acres to work with. Consequently, subjects such as space-restricted gardening and hydroponics are not covered.

YEAR ONE

GETTING STARTED

Homesteading is an idle dream for millions of Americans. They imagine themselves making a living off of the land, milking cows, and enjoying the fruits of their labors over a bountifully laden table. Most, however, never act on that impulse because getting started is so overwhelming.

The imaginations that fuel these daydreams are actually would-be farmers' worst enemies. When faced with practical reality, they begin to consider clearing land, tending to an acre of vegetables, constructing fences, feeding livestock, caring for those animals, and still making enough money to pay their bills. It's enough to deter anyone, particularly those who have limited experience with agriculture.

If I could give every aspiring homesteader a single piece of advice, it would be this: Lower your expectations and you will get there a lot faster. If you purchase 20 acres and start on one hundred different projects at once, you will run out of money and enthusiasm within a month. It's a recipe for failure.

Instead, start small. Start very small. It's unlikely that global civilization will collapse within the next few years, so take your time to adapt. Save up your money, research everything, and only begin something new when you know you have the time and funding to complete it.

It is with this principle in mind that I have divided this book into five year-long sections. Year one involves very little physical work and assumes that you are starting with no prior knowledge or infrastructure. If you have already accomplished these basic suggestions, you can move right along to year two. Otherwise, pace yourself and have patience.

Spend your first year as a homesteader reading and saving. Take local classes at a county extension office and visit the state fair. Find self-sufficiency blogs from your area to benefit from others' wisdom. You are still going to have those bewildering moments no book can account for, but when they do come along you will be better prepared to handle them if you have done your homework.

Gardening starts now, as a small plot is without question the best way to become acquainted with the basic mechanics of farming. If you are suddenly derailed by the whims of life and can no longer care for it, a garden does not suffer like animals would. Plants teach the importance of routine care, are relatively easy to keep alive, and offer a fun reward for your first year of self-sufficiency. In-depth knowledge is perhaps more useful in the long run, but there's nothing quite like tasting the first tomato that you have raised from seed to bursting red fruit.

The first step, though, is developing a game plan and a budget.

FINANCIAL PLANNING

Unless you have purchased a fully-functional farm, bringing a property up to standards takes money. There are a thousand little things that need to get done, most of which you won't even recognize until they rear their ugly heads at a crucial moment. When this happens, having something in the bank can mean the difference between a minor inconvenience and a disastrous setback.

Farmers thrive or starve by their financial sense. Droughts, disease, and insects come and go, but bills never change. As such, paying off debts and managing unavoidable expenses is just as important as pruning an orchard.

The most resource-intensive projects are fencing, housing, and completing major home renovations. Routine costs such as feed and veterinary care are a close second. All of these items can spike into five figures, but it is possible to do them yourself at a fraction of the price with some motivation and skill. Do your own work whenever possible, both to save money and to gain the experience.

Your own monthly costs should diminish as you begin to supply more of your own food and wean yourself off of the consumer mindset. Of the remaining ongoing expenses, the most important to consider is debt.

Eliminating Debt

The debt you incur in your lifetime may take up a significant portion of your paycheck. Mortgages, auto loans, credit cards, and student loans are all obligations that tie people to the consumer world and limit financial freedom. They should be avoided if at all possible.

Prevent further debt by carefully weighing the value of any new loan. Is it absolutely necessary? In some cases, such as buying a house, it's almost unavoidable. Others, like racking up credit card debt, are less excusable. Shred all but one credit card and only use the survivor for emergencies. Dealing in cash isn't always convenient, but it forces people to consider their money as a physical commodity. It is much easier to make an impulse buy by swiping plastic than counting out dollar bills.

As long as you are in debt, you are just another number in the bank's system. When you can, make extra payments to get out sooner. Financial freedom may seem almost impossible in the worst circumstances, but with the right motivation anyone can dig out of that all-too-common hole.

Reducing Spending

For the first year, getting your finances in order should be the primary goal. In lean economic times, of course, that's easier said than done.

The simplest way to identify unnecessary expenditures is to record every transaction you make in one month. If you have a smartphone, there are a number of free apps designed for this, or you can use an old-fashioned pen and notepad. Once you have your results, divide transactions into categories such as food, clothing, luxuries, restaurants, etc. It may help to create a pie chart of the final sums to visualize where your income is going.

Now, it is time to make some cuts. Total up all of the items that you *need* to survive, hold your job, and keep your finances in order. Then cut the remaining total by 75 percent. These are the luxuries, such as dining out, buying the latest gadget, or grabbing a cup of coffee on the way to work.

This is one area where the homesteading movement loses people, but you can't skip it. Being self-sufficient means being able to control yourself and choose between luxuries and stability. Older generations who still remember the Great Depression tend to have this mindset, but their descendants born into prosperity abandoned it. It's human nature to want to flaunt our wealth, but no one said human nature is sensible.

Be frugal, but don't become so uptight that buying a book or seeing that new movie is out of the question. Everything should be done in moderation, including cutting budgets. Remember that your family may not be so enthusiastic about the new rules. If you meet resistance, scale back gradually and listen to their concerns with an open mind.

Ideally, at least 10 percent of your monthly income will go into savings and only 5 percent to frivolous expenditures. The rest should be applied to bills, gasoline, groceries, and your home. Be honest with yourself, and don't fall into the habit of excusing all those tempting little purchases.

If you are already spending almost nothing on luxuries and money is still tight, you will have to be more creative with your financing and take things more slowly.

Take a year to save up as much as you can. Year one is cheap! But after that there will be things to buy on an ongoing basis, as well as the occasional emergency, and they can both make life very difficult if you don't have some cushion.

GARDENING I

Year one thankfully isn't all about deprivation. The second step toward self-sufficiency is to grow your own food with a beginner's vegetable garden. These plants are all high-yielding, easy to grow, and nutritious. You will continue growing them throughout your gardening career, as they are some of the most popular species ever cultivated.

This section assumes you are starting off in winter or early spring. If not, you may still have an abbreviated growing season before the frosts set in.

Gardening is a simple system of converting energy, nutrients, and water into usable food. On paper, there is nothing easier. As you become more proficient, you will quickly learn how many ways gardening can go wrong, as well as how to get your plants back on track without suffering total devastation.

Choosing and Starting Seeds

In later years, I recommend saving seeds in the name of sustainability and to preserve valuable strains. With that in mind, pick heritage seeds to become familiar with them early. There are hundreds of sources for seeds, including websites, catalogs, and local stores.

Once your seeds arrive, they must be started at different times to maximize their growing season. Some, like lettuce and carrots, are sown directly outdoors, but larger plants like tomatoes are usually begun indoors weeks before it is safe to transplant them.

You can buy starter trays and basic potting soil from any store with a gardening section. Don't worry about fertilizer at this stage. If you are sticking to the suggested plants, start the tomatoes, peppers, and broccoli about eight weeks before the first frost date in your area. They should all have more specific instructions on their packets.

During their time indoors, seedlings need a strong, close source of light. Invest in a grow light and either buy a stand to hang it from or make one. It should be adjustable, because the seedlings must be less than 6" away from the bulb at all times. Any further and you'll end up with "leggy seedlings," which are prone to falling over and damping off.

Plant two or three seeds in each container and thin out the smaller ones once they have germinated. Give them at least 12 hours of full light every day, but turn it off at night to let them "sleep." Keep the soil moist but not wet.

Starting seeds takes no particular skill when it comes to these hardy vegetables. If given enough light and water, they will flourish until temperatures are warm enough to move them outside. Do not do so before they develop their first pair of "adult" leaves.

Before you can subject them to the great outdoors, seedlings must be hardened off. Exposure to direct sunlight is a big shock after time under even the most powerful of grow lights. If a vulnerable young plant is simply placed outdoors, it will burn up and die.

Tolerance must be established until they are able to spend a full day in direct sun.

Start by placing seedlings outside for one hour on an overcast day. Then keep them outside for two hours the next day, three the day after that, and so on for approximately two weeks. If the plants develop yellow burns on their leaves, cut back for a few days to let them recover. When handled patiently, they should survive the transplanting process without any setbacks.

Transplanting itself is a tricky process. The easiest way is to buy biodegradable pots, which can be buried in the earth and then left to rot as the roots expand. If this is not an option, you must carefully remove the plant with as much dirt around its roots as possible and place it in its new hole without delay. Cover the roots with new dirt, water, and give the plant a few days to adjust to its new surroundings.

Location and Beds

Where a garden is located plays a major role in its overall success. You would not, for example, try to raise tomatoes in a rocky cave. An ideal spot for a garden is flat, open land with rich soil or a gentle, south-facing slope. Pick one or more promising areas and monitor them throughout the day to see which receives the most sunlight. Everything else can be adjusted, but sun exposure has to be got right the first time.

Besides sunlight, there are a few other things to consider. The garden should be close to a spigot and within sight of the house. This helps keep it a priority and makes any visiting herbivores readily apparent before they can do too much damage.

Most new garden beds begin life covered in grass. If you have several months to spare, remove it by covering the area with a tarp or newspapers. The grass underneath withers away, leaving the dirt exposed and ready for tilling. You can even dump about three inches of topsoil, compost, and organic materials on top of the grass and let it function as a mulch. By the time the seedlings are ready, the grass will have decomposed into the soil.

More advanced amending comes later, but an infusion of some compost and soil from any gardening center will suffice for now.

Stick to the basic row beds that are planted directly into the ground. Raised beds are more efficient and easier to manage, but they are just one more thing to worry about as you start cultivating your green thumb. Row beds are as simple as it gets. To save some space, have two rows of plants between every walkway, rather than a pattern of row, walkway, row, etc.

Vegetables

These vegetables are recommended for beginners just entering the world of gardening. They tend to be disease-resistant and forgiving of mistakes, while also producing family favorites in abundance.

Not everything in this section is a vegetable. Any plant that bears its seeds inside an edible shell is technically a fruit and is listed as such in the index. Since they are all grown in the traditional "vegetable garden," however, I have labeled them all as such for the purposes of this chapter.

Check online or with you cooperative extension office to find the last frost date in your county. This is the average date when frosts cease and marks the time when most plants can be moved outdoors safely.

Spacing and planting guidelines are estimates and can be adjusted as needed.

Bell Peppers

Peppers are come in all shapes, sizes, and degrees of spiciness. Bell peppers are sweet and easy to incorporate into dishes, making them a perfect first pepper in your garden. Start the seeds indoors eight weeks before the first frost date. Do not transplant until all danger of frost has passed and space them 12" apart.

Peppers are ready to harvest as little as one month after transplanting, depending on the soil quality and how much light they received while indoors.

Plants per person: 5

Square feet per plant: 1

Carrots

Carrots are crunchy, tasty, and a great source of Vitamin A. They are cold hardy and should be planted in early spring while the soil is still cool. Work the ground deeply beforehand, removing any rocks that might become obstacles to the growing root. Thin the young sprouts to 2" spacing and let them grow to your preferred size. They can remain in the soil into late fall.

Plants per person: 50

Square feet per plant: .05

Lettuce

Lettuce grows profusely and is harvested multiple times over the growing season. It is the most common leafy green found in gardens, but not the most nutritious. Plant seeds thickly in rows approximately 12" apart while the weather is still cool but not frosty. Thin to 6" spacing as plants mature. Harvest when the leaves have reached your preferred size by cutting them with a knife, promoting faster secondary growth.

Plants per person: 16

Square feet per plant: .25

Pole Beans

Pole beans are a common sight in kitchens. They come in many varieties, but the most popular are the classical long, thin green beans. Pole beans weave their way up a trellis or other support before putting on pods. If not given a trellis, they can grow up fences and even tall plants such as corn. One simple solution is to create a rectangular frame over the plants and dangle twine down to the ground. Other gardeners form teepees from wooden poles that allow more efficient plant spacing. Sow seeds directly outside once the ground is warm, spaced at 6" per plant.

Harvest the beans once they are about as thick as a pencil and snap in half with minimal effort. Do not wait long to harvest or they will become too tough.

Plants per person: 10

Square feet per plant: 1

Potatoes

Potatoes are usually consumed as French fries nowadays, but by themselves they are a delicious and versatile staple of the garden. They are one of the most nutritionally complete vegetables ever grown.

Potatoes are typically started from existing tubers. Plant them directly outdoors about two weeks before the last frost date in your area. One week before planting, place the potatoes in a warm, sunny spot to encourage sprouts. Divide each potato into sections containing two sprouts two days before planting.

Place each segment in the earth about 4" deep. Plant them 6" apart and then thin to 15" once they have poked above the surface. Potatoes are grown in mounds. Once the plant is about 10" tall, cover half of the stem and the surrounding area with dirt. Continue doing so throughout the potatoes' growing season. The plants produce flowers and then die back, and the potatoes are ready to harvest approximately two weeks afterward.

Plants per person: 10

Square feet per plant: 1.5

Spinach

Despite looking similar to lettuce, spinach is only loosely related and preferable from a nutritional standpoint. Plant seeds outdoors in early spring or late fall. Spinach thrives in cool weather and bolts, or goes to seed, in heat. Plant in rows about 12" apart and thin to 6" spacing. Work the soil beforehand to accommodate spinach's extensive roots. Harvest by cutting leaves until the plant sends up seed stalks, then pull up and sow again when the weather cools down.

Plants per person: 16

Square feet per plant: .25

Tomatoes

Tomatoes are a favorite of most gardeners, and it's not hard to see why. Home-grown tomatoes are given the opportunity to ripen on the vine and vastly superior to those orange tennis balls at the store. Start seeds indoors eight weeks before your last frost date.

Tomato seedlings are prone to legginess and damping off, so keep your light source close and ventilate well.

Once the danger of frost has passed, transplant the seedlings at 24" spacing. Place tomato cages around them for support as they grow. Time until harvest depends on the variety in question but is usually a few months.

Plants per person: 5

Square feet per plant: 2.25

Care

Plants need three basic things to survive: sunlight, water, and nutrients. For your first garden, don't worry too much about nutrients. There is plenty to learn every year, and this first harvest should provide many invaluable lessons even when kept simple.

Keep vegetables watered throughout spring and summer. Too little water kills plants or stunts output, but wet soil promotes rot and disease. As a general rule, probe the first 2" of soil with a finger every couple of days. If that first 2" is still damp, the plants are fine. If not, it's time to water. One or two long watering sessions per week are better than a short session every day.

Pluck invading weeds on sight. Don't let it get away from you; weeds take over very quickly when given the chance. It may help to lay down mulch such as straw. Mulching is covered in greater detail later.

Finally, watch for signs of blight and insects. There are many natural pests that love vegetables just as much as humans. Some bugs can be picked off by hand, like caterpillars, while others require more aggressive tactics. Releasing ladybugs will control an aphid infestation, for example.

The use of pesticides is a question you must decide on your own. Some homesteaders specifically enter the lifestyle to escape the chemicals and poisons so commonly used in industrial agriculture. On the other hand, there's no denying the appeal of being able to eliminate a bug infestation with just a few sprays. People survived thousands of years without pesticides, but it is undoubtedly more difficult and your yield may be impacted if you abstain.

Pest Control

Rabbits, birds, and deer love gardens just as much as humans do. Who wouldn't choose to sample an abundant patch of delicious and exotic greenery, especially when food is scarce elsewhere? You can choose to leave your garden open and take the losses, or you can work to deter these animal guests.

I advise against spending a small fortune on fencing in the first year, since your garden will expand later on. Instead, use a combination of inexpensive barriers and natural repellants to ward them off.

Deer and rabbits are determined creatures. Do not rely on any one strategy to keep them at bay. The following items may or may not frighten them off when laid out around the garden:

- Garlic
- Chili powder
- Blood meal
- Hair clippings
- Human, fox, or coyote urine

These methods work because of deer and rabbits' acute sense of smell. Spicy items, such as chili powder, get inhaled and irritate the sinuses, while others such as blood meal and urine alert the animals to the presence of dangerous predators. Mix your ingredients up with eggs or dish soap to adhere to surrounding foliage. They wash off in the rain and fade with time, meaning they must be reapplied at least once a week.

The problem with natural repellants is that they are unreliable. Physical barriers are more expensive but longer-lasting. Deer netting is a cheap and effective way to block access to a garden without constructing an actual fence. It can be purchased at most outdoor supply stores and then attached to surrounding branches or posts. Weigh down the bottom or stake it into the earth to keep rabbits from slipping underneath. Most nets are difficult to see and very clingy and work as much based on fear as durability.

Permanent, heavy-duty fencing for deer is a hassle and rarely 100 percent successful. Deer jump fences over seven feet high, unless they can't see through to the other side. Putting up a solid fence, however, is expensive and may limit sunlight reaching the garden. Shorter fences are made more effective by placing another fence four feet away.

YEAR TWO

EXPANDING

Think of your first year on a homestead as learning to swim in a wading pool. It's fun, hard to mess up, and a great confidence-booster. Now that you have gotten your feet wet, however, you must move on to deeper waters.

Year two explores a wider variety of topics, including the addition of fruits and livestock. These present greater demands on your time but also create a well-rounded homestead and new nutrients in your food supply.

Plan your time carefully to prevent a sudden collision of deadlines. Start building animal housing in early spring, before major work begins in the garden, and begin planting trees after transplanting your vegetables. Once the initial labor is done, maintaining everything in year two should only take up about an hour a day.

GARDENING II

Once you have a basic understanding of how plants germinate, grow, and develop produce, it's time to begin construction of a larger garden and learning about sustainable land management.

I recommend that you still grow plants in a row system, though now there must be greater attention paid to soil nutrients and quality. There are also plenty of new vegetables to add some variety to your menu. They present a few more challenges and finicky habits but are no match for the intermediate gardener.

This year, you should be able to supply at least half of your family's vegetables. Doing so requires significantly more space, but not necessarily much more time.

New Vegetables

Beets

The common garden beet is a red root packed with fiber, sugars, and essential vitamins. They are delicious when pickled or served boiled with butter. Beet greens are popular in salads and are just as healthy as the beet itself.

Sow beet seeds directly into the ground about one month before the last frost date. Soaking them one day prior to planting promotes germination. Sow them 2" apart and thin the young shoots out to 4". The thinned beets can be harvested for their leaves. The roots are harvested once they are 2" or more in diameter. Plant again in fall for a second crop.

Plants per person: 25

Square feet per plant: .15

Broccoli

Broccoli is one of the best sources of Vitamin C in the garden, but it doesn't always provide a strong harvest. If neglected or overheated, you may end up with crowns that look nothing like the broccoli seen in a grocery store. This relative of cabbages prefers cooler weather and demands special attention during the hot summer months.

Start seeds indoors eight weeks before the last frost date. Transplant at 18" spacing when the danger of frost has passed. Broccoli is prone to bolting in warm soil. Protect its root system with mulch and plenty of water.

Crowns develop as shoots from the center of the plant. Cut them off with a knife after they have reached your desired size and before they burst into flowers. Grow broccoli in both the spring and fall for two harvests.

Plants per person: 5

Square feet per plant: 2.25

Eggplant

Eggplants are great for dieters, but a poor choice for homesteaders looking to get the most bang for their buck. They are not particularly high in any nutrients or calories, making them an expendable option on this list. They are, however, a staple in many Italian recipes, a tasty meat substitute, and easy to grow.

Eggplants are related to tomatoes and grow in similar conditions. Start the seeds indoors eight weeks before the last frost date. Transplant outdoors after the last frost date at 18" spacing. Eggplants love heat and sunlight and become laden down with heavy fruits within a few months. The plants may require cages to remain upright. Harvest when the eggplants have a healthy purple sheen to them.

Plants per person: 5

Square feet per plant: 2.25

Garlic

Garlic is one of the most common seasonings used in American kitchens. This pungent bulb grows from cloves, which multiply as the garlic grows. Plant in late fall and then cover in mulch to help them weather the winter. In spring, scrape away the mulch until the sprout reaches sunlight. Each clove is placed 2" into the ground with 6" between plants.

Many garlic varieties grow curling shoots. These are called scapes, and they are cut to continue efficient bulb growth. Scapes are edible and can be incorporated into a dish just like garlic. The bulbs are ready to harvest once the lower shoots have gone brown and dry. Remove them carefully with a small trowel.

Plants per person: 15

Square feet per plant: .25

Kohlrabi

Kohlrabi is a brassica that tastes similar to mild broccoli. It grows as a hard bulb surrounded by leafy shoots. Kohlrabi can be sown outdoors, but does better when started indoors about six weeks prior to the last frost date. Some gardeners recommend as little as 6" spacing, but 12" is better.

Kohlrabi isn't fussy. If given adequate food and water the bulbs swell rapidly. Harvest when they are 2" to 3" in diameter, and peel and eat them raw or baked. Start with about five plants per person and plant again if your family likes them.

Plants per person: 10

Square feet per plant: 1

Onions

Onions are some of the most common vegetables used in cooking. Growing them from seed is a challenge, and they are most often planted as started sets instead.

Plant sets once the soil is loose enough to work. Till down to about 12" and then lightly compact the earth. Place the sets at 4" spacing, deep enough for the very tops to poke through. The onions are ready to harvest at any time, but are finished growing once the tops flop over and start to go brown.

Plants per person: 25

Square Feet per plant: .15

Radishes

Radishes are sometimes used to mark rows in a garden because they germinate so much faster than other plants. They are also a favorite snack with a strong flavor.

Work the ground to a depth of 12" before planting. Sow radish seeds two weeks before the last frost date and thin sprouts to 3" spacing. The radishes germinate within four days and mature in four weeks. Plant a new row every two weeks.

Plants per person: 25

Square feet per plant: .1

Snap Peas

Snap peas are shelled or eaten in their pod, depending on personal taste. They are one of the earliest vegetables to mature, making them a spring favorite. Like green beans, they are a climbing vine and must have some sort of trellis to support themselves.

Sow seeds outdoors one month before your local last frost date. Peas love cool temperatures and germinate quickly. Space the plants at 2" along a row and water often. Once the temperatures begin to rise, mulch the soil around the peas to keep them as cool as possible. They will continue to produce pea pods until the weather becomes too hot to tolerate.

Plants per person: 15

Square feet per plant (plus trellis): .2

Sweet Corn

Corn is a favorite for summer barbeques, overwinter storage, and livestock feed. Kernels are sowed once there is no danger of frost, as it is not a cold-hardy plant. Once the corn has sprouted, thin the shoots to 15" spacing. Corn is resource intensive.

Keep it well-watered and fertilized to develop whole and healthy ears.

Corn is ready to harvest approximately three weeks after the silks develop. Pick the ears once the kernels are plump and juicy. Most sweet corns begin to lose their flavor within days of picking and should be eaten fresh, but more primitive varieties store longer.

Plants per person: 15

Square feet per plant: 1.5

Swiss Chard

Swiss chard may look like a relative of lettuce or spinach but is actually a member of the beet family. This is one of those vegetables that people never eat before growing in the garden and then love. It is high in many nutrients, including calcium, and may even have cancer-fighting properties.

Like beets, Swiss chard seeds should be soaked for a day beforehand to boost germination rates. Space the plants at 6" and harvest once the leaves have reached your preferred size and tenderness. Cut the leaf stems with a sharp knife for faster regrowth. New leaves will be ready to harvest within a few weeks.

Plants per person: 5

Square feet per plant: .25

Turnips

The humble turnip is a cold-loving root. Plant seeds one month before your last frost date, or as soon as the soil can be worked, and two months before the winter frosts begin. Loosen the soil well before sowing.

Space turnips 4" apart and pick them once they are about 3" in diameter. Their flavor benefits from light frosts, but increased size and heat causes a woody texture. The greens are used in many recipes and popular with livestock.

Plants per person: 20

Square feet per plant: .1

Watermelons

Watermelons are not particularly nutritious and take up lots of space, but there's no denying their delectable flavor and juicy appeal in the summer months. Start watermelons indoors about eight weeks before the last frost date. Transplant them outdoors at least 24" apart and provide at least eight square feet for each plant.

Determining when a melon is ready for harvest is

a matter of experience rather than technique. Usually, the rind hardens and dulls and the stem dries out and turns brown. Cut the melon off with a sharp knife and store in a cool place until ready to eat.

Plants per person: 2

Square feet per plant: 8

Soil Amendment

Vegetables need more than just sunlight and water to grow. A garden bed is slowly depleted of vital nutrients with each successive year as plants take more and more. It is inconvenient to move a garden every few seasons, so farmers have developed ways to amend soil and keep plants productive.

First, it is important to understand the three main nutrients absorbed by plants. There are many others, of course, but for now we'll focus on the minerals used in the largest quantities.

Nitrogen (N)

Nitrogen is used to produce chlorophyll and fuels many of the energy-building processes plants use to grow. In general terms, it is responsible for healthy stem and leaf development. Plants suffering from a nitrogen deficiency are stunted and yellowish.

Phosphorous (P)

Phosphorous is also used in photosynthesis and is needed for root development. Phosphorus deficiencies manifest as bluish leaves and small, bitter produce.

Phosphorous does not appear in the soil as an independent element thanks to its chemical volatility.

Instead, it is bound to other atoms in the form of phosphates.

Potassium (K)

Potassium assists in a wide variety of functions, but is primarily another key ingredient in chlorophyll and, therefore, photosynthesis. Potassium-deficient plants have burned and blackened leaves that may be tinged with blue.

The other major minerals consumed by plants are calcium, magnesium, and sulfur, but they need less frequent amendments to remain prevalent in the soil.

Choosing a Fertilizer

Most fertilizers contain nitrogen, phosphorous, and potassium. Bags are labeled 16-16-8, 10-10-10, or something similar, indicating the percentage of each, respectively. It is also possible to buy fertilizers that supply only one nutrient.

To determine how much of each nutrient a certain garden needs, run a soil test. These can be bought as private kits or offered as a county extension office program. Your results will offer more accurate advice on what to work on, but a good general soil content is as follows:

- Phosphorous: 50-75 ppm
- Potassium: 140-175 ppm
- PH: 5.8 to 6.5[3]

Nitrogen is usually not included because it is impossible to determine how much will be available to plants throughout the growing season based on a single test. One acre of plants needs about 100 lbs of nitrogen, and up to 150 for heavy feeders like corn.[4]

Broadcast Fertilizing

Mix a complete fertilizer into the garden bed about one week prior to planting in spring. Till the fertilizer evenly into the soil, following the instructions given on the bag. Some gardeners make the mistake of thinking that more fertilizer equals more produce, but too much of any one mineral can be just as harmful as too little. Stick to the directions to promote normal plant growth.

Broadcast fertilizing gives everything in the garden a boost during the early growth stages, including weeds, but some plants need an additional feeding later on. It is no longer possible to turn up the soil at this stage, so another method called side dressing comes into play.

Side Dressing

Some plants use more minerals than others. Tomatoes, onions, potatoes, corn, watermelons, and other vegetables with long growing seasons start to lose momentum if not given a secondary source of nutrients. Side dressing takes place about one month after planting and may be continued in small doses once a month from then on.

Side dressing is accomplished by digging a shallow trench along the edge of a row, within reach of plants' roots but not so close as to damage them. The trench should be about 3" deep and extend all the way down a row. Place the fertilizer in the row and cover it with a thin coat of dirt. Water carries the fertilizer into the soil over time, ensuring that the vegetables never run short.

Organic or Inorganic Fertilizers

Besides the packaged, often inorganic, fertilizers that are easiest to use, there are also natural fertilizers that can be bought or produced at home. They are less precise but more sustainable.

The following are the most common natural fertilizers used in small gardens. How much you need to mix in depends on your soil test results.

Composted Manure

Manure and animal bedding are relatively low in nutrients compared to bagged fertilizers but add organic material to the soil, which improves water retention and mineral access. Add compost to sandy or clay soils to improve their consistency.

Poultry manure compost is the most nutrient-rich, but almost any organic matter is good matter. Other manure composts require larger volumes to have the same effect.

Bone Meal

Bone meal is a source of phosphorous and calcium made from the ground bones of livestock, typically cows. Most bone meals have an NPK rating of $4 - 21 - 0$, or similar.

Blood Meal

Blood meal is derived from the leftover blood of livestock and is very high in nitrogen. It has an NPK rating of $12 - 2 - 1$. Be careful not to over-apply this fertilizer, or it will burn the plants.

Fish Meal

Ground up fish byproducts make a good all-around fertilizer with an NPK rating around 10 – 6 – 0.

Finding What Works

Besides the kind of fertilizers you buy in a bag, there are also green manures that are grown and tilled back into the earth. I will discuss them more extensively in the future, but they include alfalfa, barley, buckwheat, clover, and rye.

It is impossible to recommend a mixture of any fertilizers because every soil is different. For the average garden, mixing in a 10 – 10 – 10 blend is unlikely to cause harm unless, of course, you dump in hundreds of pounds on a small patch. Running a test is the only way to know the deficiencies in your garden.

Natural Weed Control

Since this year sees a marked increase in your garden's square footage, controlling weed growth becomes more important. Many new gardeners bite off more than they can chew and end up overwhelmed by weeds, their plants withered away somewhere underneath a tangle of grass and vines.

Start the season with aggressive weed control to prevent this scenario. Mulch is any material placed over the ground to inhibit the growth of plants. There are several different types of mulch, each with their own benefits and drawbacks.

Black Plastic

Plastics are the most reliable mulches. They are laid over a patch of ground, weighed down with another mulch, and then cut into when a plant is placed into the soil. Plastics heat up the ground, making them a poor choice for gardens with cool-loving plants like broccoli, peas, or spinach. They also lower water absorption.

Newspapers

Newspapers act in a similar fashion as plastic, but they let more water through to the roots below and build up less heat. Stack the newspapers eight sheets high in overlapping rectangles. They blow away if not secured by another mulch. Popular combinations include grass clippings, straw, or bark. Only use black and white paper.

Straw

Straw is one of the best mulches available. It should not be fresh, or you will end up with an invasion of grains to rival any noxious weed. It is also adored by rodents in the winter and may become infested if left in the bed. Till it into the soil at the end of the growing season to add more organic material and leave small critters homeless.

Grass Clippings

Grass clippings are a controversial mulch. They are effective, natural, and are even a good fertilizer as they break down and join the soil. On the other hand, the added nitrogen can burn plants, and grass may heat up the ground as it decomposes. Green grass is applied in the early spring, several weeks before transplanting, and should be considered a fertilizer. Later on, when the mulch needs updating, use brown grasses that have little nutritional value.

Bark

The standard mulch for landscaping is made of

chips of bark, but it should be avoided in a vegetable garden. Some bark is acidic, and decomposing wood removes nitrogen from the soil.

Cardboard

Cardboard is similar to newspaper in that it allows water to enter the soil while presenting a physical barrier for young weeds. Also like newspaper, it should be combined with another mulch.

Leaves

Leaves are an abundant natural mulch, but you have to gather them in the fall to have a ready supply in spring. Store the leaves in a dry environment. They have a tendency to blow away, so mulch thick or pair it with newspapers and cardboard. Chop the leaves up beforehand for a more attractive and uniform appearance.

As a general rule, don't rely on any one form of mulch to keep the garden free of weeds. Find what is most available in your own circumstances, and be sure to pluck any weeds that slip through before they become a problem.

Composting

This year marks the introduction of livestock, which means your homestead is going to start accumulating manure and pine shavings in surprising volume. Both contain valuable nutrients and balance each other nicely in a compost pile.

Composting is the process of turning waste materials into a rich organic mixture resembling soil. Compost improves the quality of soil consistency as well as adding nitrogen and other elements. A healthy compost pile generates plenty of heat and is a thriving culture for decomposing bacteria.

Compost Bins

Compost should be stored in bins, rather than lumped into a pile, unless your operation is truly massive.

A compost bin is well ventilated and holds at least 25 cubic feet. Wood pallets are a plentiful building material, as are plastic barrels with holes punched along the sides. The easiest bin of all is a circle made of welded wire fencing, which may be the most effective in terms of ventilation.

There are also bins available for sale, but you're going to need more than one and the costs add up quickly.

Composing Compost

There are four primary ingredients to a good compost heap: carbon, nitrogen, water, and oxygen. The first two make up the vast majority of the mixture and are referred to as brown and green materials.

The Brown (Carbon)

Carbon is the fuel that feeds the organisms breaking down the green materials. It includes any dry plant matter such as wood shavings, leaves, straw and brown grass clippings. Most farms with livestock have an easy supply of brown compost through pine shavings and straw.

The Green (Nitrogen)

Nitrogen is what makes compost so valuable. Green compost materials are made up of fresh organic matter like manure, green grass clippings, and kitchen scraps.

Water

A compost bin does not need to be kept soaking wet, but it should remain damp. Most bins exposed to normal rainfall will be sufficiently hydrated.

Oxygen

Oxygen is necessary for life to survive within a compost heap, as it is almost everywhere else. It is mixed in through adequate ventilation and timely turning of the pile.

Composting is not a precise science, but it does require some care. An improper ratio of browns and greens will leave you with little more than a dead pile or useless sludge.

Aim for about 50 – 75 percent brown compost and 25 – 50 percent green by weight, not volume. It may help to weigh things out at first, but most gardeners eventually develop a good feel for feeding their compost bins.

Think of the compost bin as a living organism. It is, in fact, made up of colonies of bacteria. A live bin is hot at the center and produces a thick, loamy substance. If a bin is cold and dead, but has true compost at the center, it needs to be turned. Use a pitchfork or shovel to mix and shuffle the bin's contents.

If that doesn't work, reassess the compost's ratios and aeration. Add some green matter to get it cooking again and toss in a handful of dirt to introduce the necessary microbes.

Add compost two weeks before planting. This gives it time to integrate with the soil and begin spreading nutrients.

What to Avoid

Some items do more harm than good and should not be placed in a compost pile. Meats, dairy, and bread draw in hungry scavengers. Avoid using any wood unless you know that it is untreated. Do not add human feces or the feces of cats and dogs.

Basically, if something came from a healthy plant or out of an herbivore's backside, it should be alright to add in. Shun carnivorous manure and other animal byproducts, with the exception of poultry droppings.

Composts are a sustainable resource that can significantly improve your crop yields and save money on other fertilizers. As you add more livestock and use up produce from your garden, return your unused nutrients to the earth to become one step closer to self-sufficiency.

ORCHARDS I

The average American consumes 280 pounds of fruit per year.[5] It's not hard to see why; fruits are delicious and a natural source of sugar, calories, and vital nutrients. The only trouble is that those sugars cause them to decompose far more rapidly than the typical vegetable. Thanks to canning, however, an orchard can supply a family with safely preserved fruits for the entire year.

Growing fruits is a completely different game than vegetables. Certainly there are similarities. The plants need all of the same nutrients as before, but they have their own quirks, cycles, diseases, and maintenance. They tend to be perennials, capable of producing abundant fruits every year for decades.

The problem with perennials is that you cannot

make the same mistakes with an orchard that you can with a garden. A vegetable garden that underwhelms only staggers on for a year before you can correct your mistakes and do better the next time. A tree that is poorly tended or in the wrong climate disappoints for half a lifetime. Before you start planting, ensure that you are really ready to make the commitment.

Two types of fruit are covered in this section: those that grow on trees and those that grow on vines, bushes, and brambles. Both have a place in any orchard, and both require careful planning to gain maximum yields. Besides fruits, I also recommend nut trees, which once covered vast swaths of North America and provide hundreds of pounds of protein for the winter.

Planning an Orchard

A self-sufficient orchard takes space, but not necessarily a large chunk of land. If you are lacking in acreage, replace your landscaping trees with fruiting ones. It's better to have a dedicated area for an orchard, simply because it's easier to tend to and harvest, but plant trees anywhere you have space. They are the ultimate permaculture, and the more you have the better off you will be.

First, homesteaders need to know what they can grow. Those in the Southern states are in luck, because the longer the growing season, the more trees there are available. Some species, on the other hand, need a period of winter dormancy and will not produce fruits in frost-free zones.

Grow as many different varieties as you can and plant at least one new tree every year. Late frosts will kill any buds on the trees, so keep a wide selection.

Dwarf Trees vs. Standards

Before you begin planning out an orchard, determine which type of trees you will grow. Dwarf trees are becoming more popular among both small and industrial farms because of their reduced spacing requirements, but they also need more careful handling and are vulnerable to disease. The typical dwarf tree is 50 to 70 percent smaller than a standard.

At the other end of the spectrum, standard-sized trees are big. If allowed to grow unimpeded, they reach heights of 30 feet or more, with a diameter of another 30 feet. They can be pruned, but harvesting even a perfectly tended standard tree is a real chore. In exchange, they produce massive harvests and are hardier than the smaller varieties.

There's also a middle road: the semi-dwarf. Semi-dwarfs are 30 to 40 percent smaller than standards and middling in terms of production and hardiness. In most circumstances, the semi-dwarf is more than sufficient without reaching the dangerous heights of standards. Your local county extension office will be able to tell you which varieties of each tree do best in your area. The fruits listed in the next section cover expected yields and spacing for all three sizes when available.

Fruit Trees

These are the most common fruit varieties cultivated in the United States.

Apples

Apples are a staple of nearly every homestead. They are hardy and produce abundant, sweet fruits that store well. There are thousands of varieties to choose from. Different apples ripen at different times, have different colors, and are resistant to different climates and diseases. They range in size from five feet tall to 30.

Most apple trees cross-pollinate, meaning they require another variety nearby to form healthy, numerous fruits. Besides viable genetic material, they also need a pollinator, typically bees. Plant two separate varieties with a similar bloom time within 100 feet of each other for best results. Crab apple trees are often used for this purpose because they have long flowering periods. The quality of pollination in apples can be ascertained by counting the number of seeds at their core. A well-pollinated apple has approximately seven seeds. The fewer the seeds the less fertile the apples, and the less likely they are to make it to harvest.

Plant apple trees in spring, after the last frost date. Spread compost or aged manure under the branches once a year to provide nutrients for the tree. Depending on its size, an apple tree takes anywhere from two to eight years to begin producing. Adult standard trees have a lifespan of approximately 40 years.

The following numbers are a general estimate of yields and spacing by size, as provided by the University of Tennessee.[6] Individual performance varies by location, growing conditions, and variety.

Tree Size	Bushels Per Tree	Square Ft. Per Tree
Dwarf	1 ½	84
Semi-Dwarf	6	384
Standard	10	600

Apricots

Apricots are similar to peaches and come in all three sizes, from potted dwarf plants to 25-foot-tall standard trees. Apricots require a dormant winter period and are hardy up to Zone 4. Purchase a disease-resistant variety, as they are vulnerable to several major infections. Most apricots need another variety nearby to be pollinated, but there are self-pollinizing types available.

Apricots are finicky trees that do not always respond well to human intervention. Prune very lightly during the first two years, only removing branches that are too vertical or that intersect a better branch. Trim away new growth, or suckers, that sprout around the main trunk. Prune in the summer on a dry day; pruning in the winter leaves the tree open to infection. Provide a light layer of mulch around the roots and don't fertilize heavily.

Apricots and other stone fruits are prone to disease, meaning they must be watched carefully for signs of mildew and open sores along the branches and trunk.

Tree Size	Bushels Per Tree	Square Ft. Per Tree
Dwarf	1	100
Semi-Dwarf	2	200
Standard	3	400

Cherries

Cherries are a perennial favorite for their distinctive flavor and small size. They come in two main types: sweet and pie.

Sweet cherries are the kind used for raw consumption, but they are more prone to disease and less hardy. They produce fruits after six years, come in all size varieties, and are easy to train as they grow.

Pie cherries are bitter and only suitable for pies or canning. On the other hand, they are wilder than their sweet cousins and hardy to Zone 4. They require less room and suffer from fewer diseases.

There are also wild cherries, which are the toughest of all and can grow nearly anywhere, such as black cherries and chokecherries. The fruits of chokecherries are edible, but their leaves and pits are toxic.

Cherries typically cross-pollinate and begin producing within three to six years.

Tree Size	Pounds Per Tree	Square Ft. Per Tree
Semi-Dwarf	60	400
Standard	80	500

Peaches and Nectarines

Peaches and nectarines are closely related stone fruits particularly popular in the South. Unfortunately, these trees take almost any excuse to falter and die. A mild winter can halt fruit production, while late frosts destroy the buds. Diseases are common. They also have shorter lifespans than other fruit trees and rarely make it to 20 years old.

Plant them with native soil and spread the roots out as far as possible. Prune in an open style for better air circulation, trim the sapling down to 36", and cut off the side branches after planting. Branches should then be shaped up and out, with no major central shoot.

Peaches are highly prone to disease and infestation. Any signs of diseases such as leaf curl, scab, and mildew must be treated aggressively, and most abundant harvests are reliant on insecticides. Organic peaches are nearly impossible to grow consistently but should provide small, steady harvests. Thin peach fruits as they grow to 6" spacing. Otherwise the limbs become overburdened and snap under the weight of their load.

Tree Size	Bushels Per Tree	Square Ft. Per Tree
Semi-Dwarf	3	320
Standard	5	480

Pears

Pears are easier to grow than stone fruits but still prone to a few problems. They are a sweet, slightly dry fruit that stores well. Pear trees range in size from 12 feet to 40 and are hardy in Zones 4 – 9

Plant saplings and prune gently for the first few years. Pears do not respond well to pruning and should only be trimmed mildly. Most varieties cross-pollinate.

Common pears are harvested before they are ripe, just as they start to lighten in color and are easy to pull from the branches. Keep the pears in a cool location to let them finish ripening. Doing so prevents premature falls and rot.

Tree Size	Bushels Per Tree	Square Ft. Per Tree
Dwarf	1	180
Semi-Dwarf	2	400
Standard	3	600

Plums

Plums resemble smaller, tarter peaches and nectarines. They are durable, hardy trees that persevere where others fail. Plum trees reach only 20 feet in height, and varieties are available that can produce anywhere from Zone 2 to 9.

Prune plums gently as they grow and do not remove the thin fruiting branches. Many types self-pollinize, but plant two varieties within 50 feet of each other to improve fertility. Trees begin producing within three or four years. Harvest the plums when they can be picked easily and are soft to the touch.

Tree Size	Bushels Per Tree	Square Ft. Per Tree
Semi-Dwarf	2	320
Standard	3	480

Nut Trees

Nut trees are overshadowed by their flashy fruit counterparts, but they are just as important on a homestead. They are a reliable source of fats and proteins when they reach maturity, though some like to say that farmers plant nuts for their grandchildren.

The true definition of a nut is somewhat shaky, but for all intents and purposes I have grouped any hard but edible produce of a tree in this section. Trees that require an extreme Southern climate have been omitted, such as peanuts.

Almonds

Almonds are a relative of the peach, though their fruit is smaller and inedible. Most almonds in America are grown in California because of their early blooms and subsequent need for a mild climate. They prefer Zone 7 to 9, but some may survive in Zone 6.

Plant grafts early in the spring to encourage strong roots. The soil should have a neutral pH and be full of organic materials to keep it well drained. Every spring thereafter, give the tree a dose of fertilizer to help it along. Water once a week during the first year.

Almond trees are relatively compact but should be spaced approximately 25 feet apart. Many almonds can self-pollinize, but others need another variety close by. Prune dead or sickly branches and maintain a well-ventilated interior as the almond tree grows.

Grafted trees should begin producing within four years and produce at least 30 pounds of nuts per year. Harvest when the hulls have turned black and receded from the nut, typically in August or September.

Chestnuts

Chestnuts were once a common sight in the United States and covered much of its forested lands. Unfortunately, an imported blight has all but destroyed the standard American chestnut, and the massive trees now lay stunted in the soil. Today, most varieties sold in America are blight-resistant.

Chestnuts need organic soils with a pH between 5 and 6.5. They grow in Zones 4 to 8. Plant more than one variety to cross-pollinate. The most common varieties in use today are Chinese chestnuts, but there are also European, Japanese, and blight-resistant American chestnuts to choose from.

Chestnuts are very large trees and need at least 30 feet of spacing, with 40 or more preferable. Smaller types can be kept at 20 foot spacing with diligent pruning. They grow quickly and reach heights of 60 feet or more.

The Chinese chestnut begins production in around five years; others may take longer. A fully grown chestnut tree can produce over 250 pounds of nuts[7], which are traditionally harvested as they drop.

Hazelnuts

Hazelnuts are a small nut commonly seen in mixes at the store but rarely sold on their own. They have a sweet, woody flavor and are ground up as a flavor additive. Coffee and chocolate with hazelnuts are a delicious treat.

The American varieties are hardy from Zones 4 to 9. They resemble bushes more than trees, often reaching a mere 10 feet in height, and should be encouraged to grow like a shrub.

Plant saplings in early spring at 10-foot spacing. Hazelnuts need another variety to pollinize each other. Lightly prune back new suckers and fertilize once a year to keep them growing in an orderly manner.

It will be at least four years before a started

sapling begins producing hazelnuts. They usually ripen in the fall and drop to the ground. Harvest quickly, as they are a favorite of birds and squirrels. Place the nuts in water and throw out any that float. A fully grown hazelnut tree produces about 10 pounds per year,[8] though some yield more.

Hickories

President Andrew Jackson was nicknamed "Old Hickory;" his protégé President James Polk was subsequently called "Young Hickory." These titles were an allusion to the toughness of hickory wood, which is still prized to this day and also used to smoke meats and other foods.

Hickories grow to be 80 feet tall and produce nuts similar to pecans. They are hardy in Zones 4 to 9. Hickories are somewhat unappreciated today, but they are a useful tree for their shade, wood and ample supply of nuts. Plant two trees of different varieties next to each other at 25 foot spacing. They are an upright tree and shouldn't crowd each other. The most popular types for nuts are shagbark and shellbark hickories.

Hickories planted as saplings begin giving nuts in three years.

Pecans

Pecans are closely related to hickories but need a warmer climate. They are one of the most popular nuts on the market, but they are also space-intensive, growing to 100 feet tall and 60 feet wide, and prone to disease. In exchange, the nuts are tender, sweet, and prolific.

Pecans survive in Zones 5 to 9. Plant them with at least 50-foot spacing and use two different varieties for pollination. Water young trees several times a week and fertilize once a year. Prune saplings gently to promote stronger roots and trunks.

Pecans are large trees and take a while to hit full production. Grafted saplings start dropping nuts in less than five years. A fully grown pecan tree yields an average of 40 or 50 pounds per tree.[9] The nuts ripen in fall and can be collected like any other nut tree.

Walnuts

Black walnut trees grow wild and flourish on the East Coast, but farms elsewhere in the nation have to grow their own. The most common types in America are the English (or Persian) and black walnut.

English walnuts are seen in stores because of their thinner shells and looser meat. They need warm climates, but Carpathians are hardy up to Zone 5.

Black walnuts can be grown in Zone 4 and are also valued for their beautiful wood. A sizable copse of well-tended black walnut trees is worth millions of dollars. They are named black walnuts because of the inky fluid excreted by their hulls. This will stain clothing, hands, and even concrete. The nuts themselves are harder than English walnuts and have a slightly "wilder" flavor.

Most walnut trees self-pollinize and need at least 20 feet of spacing. Keep the sapling watered during its first few years. Walnut trees are producers of juglone, in both their leaves and roots, which is toxic to other plants. This is an effective survival adaptation for the trees, but it means you must give your other vegetation a wide berth.

A walnut tree should begin producing nuts about four years after planting a sapling. The nuts look like round, green fruits and blacken and drop off the tree when they are ready for harvest.

Bushes and Vines

Not every fruit grows on a tree. There are multitudes of other plants that produce delicious and nutrient-packed fruits, most notably grapes and berries. Each plant is unique, but they all make valuable additions to the farm.

Blackberries

Blackberries are relatives of the raspberry and have similar thorny vines. Some areas, such as the Pacific Northwest, have an abundance of them growing wild, and local farmers might laugh at the concept of willfully growing this pest. Blackberry season, however, always brings out families willing to brave the thorns for the tart, juicy fruits.

Domestic blackberries have many names: blackberry, loganberry, dewberry, boysenberry, and more. Some are simply different varieties, others are hybrids. They all, however, have roughly the same growing needs. They prefer soil at a pH of 6.0 to 7.0

with plenty of nutrients.

Use a trellis system as with raspberries, or let them grow up on themselves to form a hedge. The latter is less efficient and more difficult to manage, but it still creates a ready supply of berries and forms a solid natural barrier against pests.

Plant blackberries three feet apart with seven feet between rows. They should begin to bear fruit in their second year. The berries are ready to eat when they are sweet and juicy, typically starting in June.

Square feet per plant: 15

Plants per person: 3

Blueberries

Blueberries are widely considered to be a "super food" because they are an abundant source of Vitamin C, antioxidants, fiber, and a host of other vitamins and minerals. They have anti-aging and anti-cancer properties and also happen to be one of the best-tasting berries available. When grown properly, they produce many fruits and are a highlight of any gardener's growing season.

Plant blueberry bushes in acidic soils at pH 4.5 – 5.5. Check the pH every year and add more acidic materials as needed. This process is covered later on in the chapter. The most common varieties need a winter dormancy period and warm, humid summers, but there are now new types available with extended ranges.

Plant several different varieties together for cross-pollination. Prune old growth and long branches back early in the spring each year. Most blueberries begin bearing fruit in three years and hit full production at five. They begin to ripen in June and some carry through as late as September. The best varieties, if cared for properly, produce eight to 10 pounds per plant.[10]

Square feet per plant: 16

Plants per person: 3

Raspberries

Raspberries grow successfully in the wild across much of the United States, but the domesticated varieties provide more and larger fruits. Like many other berries, they are highly nutritious. Raspberries are a sprawling, thorn-covered vine that can be trained up a trellis or allowed to sprawl across other plants. Guiding them is preferable when it comes time to harvest. Raspberry varieties are hardy in Zones 3 to 10.

Raspberries are difficult to get wrong. In fact,

you're more likely to spend a few hours each summer cutting back their new canes than struggling to help them thrive. Plant them in well-drained soil with a pH of about 6 with approximately three foot spacing between plants and seven feet between rows. They should be grown under a trellis to support their heavy fruits and keep them contained.

Add fertilizer to the raspberries every year, but do not apply it less than 4" from the plants themselves. In the late winter, cut back dead growth to make way for younger, more efficient canes.

Berries are ready to harvest when they have reached their natural color, typically red, and can easily be pulled from the plant.

Square feet per plant: 15

Plants per person: 3

Strawberries

Strawberries are the most common fruits found in a garden. They are a favorite among children and adults alike thanks to their large fruits and sweet flavor. They are shorter-lived than most other plants in the orchard and need maintenance similar to vegetables. In fact, they are often grown in a vegetable bed.

There are three main varieties of strawberries. The

traditional June-bearing plants put on fruit for less than a month, but their berries are large and produced in great numbers. Ever-bearing fruits have two or three harvest periods throughout the year, but tend to have smaller and fewer berries each time. Day neutral strawberries have a constant supply of fruit, at the expense of size and flavor. The latter two are much less space intensive than June-bearing varieties.

Started strawberries are planted about 24" apart in rows. Raised beds are useful for containing them and can be used as a permanent strawberry patch.

Remove the buds of June-bearing strawberries during the first year to foster stronger growth. Everbearing and day neutral plants can be allowed to set flowers after June. From then on, strawberries should provide prolific fruits for three years, possibly four. It's wise to have two different strawberry beds in constant rotation to cover the replanting periods.

Managing runners and only allowing carefully chosen daughter plants improves yields but takes more careful management. Many strawberry patches end up a mess of runners without weekly care.

Square feet per plant: 1 with runners

Plants per person: 10

Grapes

Growing grapes is an ancient tradition on farms. Historically they have been primarily used to create wine, but many modern homesteaders also grow them for fresh eating and canning. Each variety, and there are many, is suited to a unique climate. Call your extension office to learn which types are suited for your county.

There are two types of grapes: table and wine. Table grapes, the kind you buy at the store, are big, fat, and often seedless. Wine grapes are smaller and tarter.

Grow grape plants along rows of trellis, typically two strands of wire staked at 15 foot intervals. Once the grapes have reached the strands, allow the main trunk to thicken and strengthen, but limit limb growth.

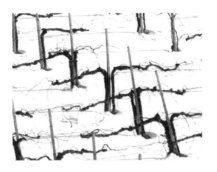

Some vineyards give their grapes four main branches, one stretching out on either side of the plant along two wires. Others grow only along the top strand, as shown on the previous page.

Both methods promote channeling nutrients into the grapes rather than wasting energy toward new growth. Every winter, cut the old shoots down to those two or four arms, leaving spurs in place.

With the right support and management, grapes should produce multiple clusters for decades. A well-tended plant can grow 15 pounds of grapes per year.[11] Do not harvest grapes when they change colors. It takes another couple of weeks for them to develop the proper sugars and nutrients.

Square feet per plant: 35

Plants per person: 3

Planting Trees

A typical family only needs two or three of each fruit tree, but plant as many as you can. Not only will the different varieties have different harvesting seasons, keeping fresh fruit available for more months of the year, but they also protect against crop failure. After all, in the event of a true disaster it is better to have too much food than too little.

It takes most trees three to five years to begin real production, and many are not fully grown for a decade or more. That is why I recommend that you begin this undeniably large undertaking in year two. The sooner they are in the ground the sooner you can benefit from them. If the expenses start adding up, limit yourself to a few trees a year in staggered plantings.

Starting Seeds vs. Transplanting

It is better to start an orchard with cuttings from proven, established trees. These cuttings are strong and healthy, making them perfect for beginners and preferred even by the experts. They need only be planted in the ground and given adequate care to grow.

Seeds, meanwhile, are a mixed bag. They may not always germinate or survive the initial growing process. Some seeds need to lie dormant for years before they germinate. When they do reach full growth, they often perform worse than their cut counterparts. They are, however, much cheaper. If you are truly dedicated to natural, sustainable living, plant an orchard of heritage seeds. Otherwise, stick with cuttings and you won't need to worry about propagation for at least 15 years.

Planting a sapling is not difficult. Dig a hole large enough to hold the roots without bending them back on themselves. Use a shovel or another tool to loosen the soil at the edges. This makes it easier for the roots to expand later. Place the tree in the hole so that the roots are entirely covered. The sapling will have what is known as a graft union near its base, which resembles a ring around the stem. This union should be three inches above the soil level.

Keep the saplings well watered during the early stages. Proper soil is damp but not wet. In time, most trees survive on nothing but rain water.

Deterring Pests

Even more so than vegetables, trees and other fruit-bearing plants are prone to pests. You will, at some point, run into a problem with animals in your orchard. The trick is knowing how to discourage them before losing your entire crop or, worse, decades-old trees.

Pests tend to remain the same everywhere: deer, bugs, and birds. Rodents and dogs also pose a hazard.

Insects

Insects are abundant and often specialized to live off of certain trees. They drill, chew, invade, and invariably lay eggs to spawn the next generation. Watch especially for moths, caterpillars, and aphids. Insecticides are the most efficient way to kill bugs. Organic operations remove them by hand, use pheromones to disrupt breeding, release beneficial insects, and graze flocks of poultry in the orchard to consume larvae.

Deer

When food becomes scarce, deer turn to orchards. They pick up fallen fruits, nibble new shoots, and in the winter they even peel off bark. Deer can kill trees if left to their own devices. Use tall fencing (at least eight feet high) or plant a barrier of blackberries and raspberries around the orchard. Wrap young trees with chicken wire or apply deterrents to the trunk if problems persist. A good dog left in the orchard will also be able to scare off most deer.

Birds

Birds keep insect populations down, but they also love berries just as much as we do. Throw some netting over plants while the berries are forming to keep the birds at bay. Sparkling streamers frighten unwary birds, but canny individuals get over them quickly.

Rodents and Rabbits

Rodents and rabbits are rarely a problem, but they can damage roots and trunks if desperate. An outdoor cat or a terrier helps keep the population down, otherwise use traps to control them.

Diseases

Besides animals, the other major impact on orchard performance is disease. All trees are susceptible to damage and infection, but stone fruits like peaches are often the hardest-hit.

Stricken trees are more than just ugly. They are inefficient. A disease that isn't virulent enough to kill can still effectively halt fruit production, which is why it's so important to catch symptoms early. Inspect your orchard every few weeks for any worrisome changes, and take immediate action when a disease does infiltrate your trees.

There are too many diseases in the United States alone to list them all here, but these are some of the most common:

Bacterial Canker

Bacterial canker is caused by two different types of bacteria, but the symptoms are the same. It is most often seen on plums and cherries. Trees develop sunken, oozing wounds. If allowed to spread, these cankers kill entire branches and eventually the tree itself. Treat with aggressive pruning in late summer, leaving only healthy wood behind. Spray with a copper-based fungicide to finish it.

Black Knot

Black knot, pictured above, is another stone-fruit disease affecting plums, cherries, prunes, and to a lesser extent peaches and apricots. It is easy to identify based on the black, tumorous growths that encroach upon smaller branches and finally spread to the trunk itself. The most effective treatment is one of aggressive pruning and periodic fungicide applications.

Black Rot

Black rot can describe a number of conditions, but in this case is referring to the disease that impacts apples and pears. It is a bacterial infection that causes brown, mushy spots on fruits. The fruits remain on the tree and do not fall apart, but they are rendered inedible.

Brown Rot

Where black rot is bacterial, brown rot is a fungus. It causes cankers, rotten fruit, and stunted performance. Affected fruits develop characteristic puffs of fungus. Remove any damaged fruits and branches and treat with a fungicide.

Fire Blight

Fire blight is perhaps the most serious disease that can hit apples and pears. It is a bacterial infection that makes leaves look as though they have been scorched. They wither and blacken, leaving bare branches and no way for the tree to gather vital sunlight. The fruit is small and covered in dark spots, and cankers form along the branches. Fire blight kills quickly. Treat with bactericide and buy cultivars that are disease-resistant.

Leaf Curl

Leaf curl occurs in peaches and is caused by a fungus. It harms performance, first manifesting as red spots on leaves. The leaves develop a curl as they grow before being overcome by the fungus. Although trees grow new leaves after the curled ones are shed, the wasted resources harm the peach crop. Fungicides and extra nitrogen may be able to limit the damage.

Powdery Mildew

Powdery mildew is yet another fungal infection describing the condition of many plants. It is quickly diagnosed based on the light, powdery coating of mildew on the leaves of apples and pears. Although genetic resistance is being promoted in cultivation, fungicides are necessary to combat the infection.

Scab

Scab appears most commonly on apples and manifests as black splotches on the surface of the fruit. The scabs are relatively harmless, but they look ugly and should be cut off the apple when eaten raw. Treat with fungicides.

Pruning

Once they have been given access to nutrients, water, and sunlight, trees and bushes usually begin growing enthusiastically. In fact, they sometimes grow too enthusiastically. A tree allowed to develop naturally may mature into an inefficient provider.

Pruning should not be undertaken lightly. It is the fundamental shaping of a living being, and a single cut branch can change a tree's output for the rest of its life or even kill it. Think very carefully before removing any limb, because there is no going back.

Always wash and sanitize your pruning tools to prevent the spread of fungi and bacteria. Pruning guides a tree into a strong shape, determined by its species. Common strategies throughout are removing weak limbs and improving overall ventilation, ease of access, and structural integrity.

Remove limbs as close to the tree as possible without damaging the trunk itself. The connecting section is called a bark collar and should be preserved to speed up healing.

Prune once a year to train growth. Late winter is the most practical time because it gives a clear view of the tree and occurs during a dormant period. Begin by removing dead, upright, or crowded limbs. They are the primary sources of trouble during the growing season. Also aggressively remove any signs of disease or infestation.

The two pruning styles are central leader and open center. Trees in the open-center style are pictured above. A central-leader tree looks something like a Christmas tree. Open-center pruning promotes ventilation and is easier to care for and harvest. Central leaders grow tall and strong.

Open center is the preferred method for many trees, especially stone fruits. In the end, however, it is largely a matter of your personal taste and habits. Many trees need almost no pruning whatsoever. Experiment, make a few mistakes, and get a feel for what you like.

POULTRY I

A vegetarian can get by on fruits and vegetables, but the average family craves protein and prefers to get the bulk of it from animal by-products. Notably, the average American ate 86 pounds of chicken in 2006. [12] Chickens are the quintessential farm animal because they produce two different foods, meat and eggs, on limited resources. Both eggs and meat are sustainable, nutritious, and far tastier when raised through traditional practices.

The chicken in the grocery aisle is not your grandmother's chicken and, from a phenotypic perspective, bears a greater resemblance to the turkeys of a hundred years ago. They are massive, bloated, and packed with breast meat. They reach slaughter weight in six to eight weeks and use astonishingly little feed for every pound gained.

This business model is excellent for the poultry industry, but not so much for the millions of chickens currently being raised in warehouses across the nation. They are plagued with health issues, and many do not make it to eight weeks. Their feed must be limited or they literally eat themselves to death. Their bodies cannot support their growth and it's common for the breast meat to atrophy into greenish goo. Their legs break, their hearts give out, and if left in the sun they will die of heat exhaustion rather than move into the shade.

If they survive to breeding age, usually through severely restricted feeding, they are often too ungainly to mate and the hens produce few eggs. The offspring do not reach the same weights as their parents, because the parents themselves are hybrids. Such is the modern broiler.

The story of the egg industry is a similar one, and just as cruel. Egg-laying hens are also specially developed hybrids, kept in cages to never see the light of day. Many have their beaks clipped to prevent the cannibalism and egg-breaking associated with living in stressed and cramped conditions.

Hens living in 'cage-free' environments are kept in the same large warehouses, only in the name of humanity they are able to scramble about in a tightly packed hoard of other chickens. If they have access to the outdoors, it is in a small enclosed balcony with mesh windows. Virtually all eggs sold at the grocery store come from these conditions: The average American eats 250 per year.[13]

The entire process of domestication is based on the concept of exploiting animals for their resources. That often means raising them for the express purpose of slaughter. At some point, however, respect got taken out of the equation. When people abandoned their backyard flocks for the convenience of the store, they paved the way for an industrial takeover that has resulted in untold and unseen misery for billions of animals.

The move toward traditional poultry farming emerged after the public became aware of the conditions their food is being raised in. In the past decade, chicken ownership has expanded throughout the nation. They are the easiest of all livestock to maintain and can be kept on even the smallest of properties.

For your first year raising chickens, I advise focusing on eggs alone. Because laying is a natural part of chicken biology, it is a simple way to learn the basics of these animals while still getting a return on your investment.

Like any livestock, chickens have three basic needs: food, water, and shelter. Before you pick up your first batch of chicks, you must be prepared to care for them every day.

Popular Backyard Breeds

Choosing a chicken breed is an exciting process for first-time owners. These birds have been shaped by mankind for thousands of years to suit every taste and utility. They range from fluffy little bantams to lanky, primitive Orientals with a huge spectrum in between.

There are three basic kinds of chicken: egg-layers, broilers, and dual-purpose. Dual-purpose breeds are kept for both meat and eggs, but are not top producers of either. Layers and broilers have been bred to be unmatched at their specialties, but they serve little purpose for anything else and are unable to breed true. Dual purpose birds are essential for sustainable living, but many families also use broilers and laying hybrids alongside them. These are the most popular dual-purpose breeds.

Australorp

The Australorp is, as its name suggests, an Australian breed developed primarily from Orpingtons. It is a large, black bird with soft feathers. An Australorp holds the world record of 364 eggs laid in 365 days. Most, however, can be expected to produce an average of 250 eggs per year.

Well-bred Australorps make good table birds and have docile personalities. Their dark plumage leaves harmless black pigment in carcass' skin that some consider unappealing, but it also helps them avoid the attention of predators.

Cochin

The Cochin is largely kept as an ornamental breed and a popular choice for families with children. They take some time to fill out and produce less than 200 eggs per year. On the other hand, they make for large and flavorful meals and are renowned broody hens. A few Cochins in the flock will hatch and raise new generations without incubators.

Cochins are recognized by their feathered legs and profusion of soft feathers and down. They are a friendly breed, and their charm makes up for their lackluster laying performance.

Easter Egger

Easter Eggers are commonly sold labeled as Ameracaunas or Aracaunas but are in fact a mix of several breeds. Their defining characteristic is their blue and green eggs. Most also have muffs, or beard-like feathers surrounding the face, and small pea-combs. They are a hardy, slender type and not particularly suitable as meat birds.

Because they do not conform to any standards, Easter Eggers come in many shapes and sizes. They produce 150 to 250 eggs per year with colors ranging from light blue to a dark, olive green.

Leghorn

Leghorns were the go-to laying breed for centuries. They are light birds with flighty temperaments. Leghorns are rarely friendly and tend to be the escape artists of a flock, but in exchange, they produce as much as 300 large white eggs every year.

Leghorns have been bred to discourage broodiness and almost never sit on eggs. They make for scrawny dinners, but a few processed batches of cockerels per year are more than enough to feed a family.

Marans

Marans are a dual-purpose breed renowned for both their superior meat and extremely dark eggs. A quality Marans hen will lay eggs the shade of chocolate syrup. They are smaller than some other breeds but fill out more quickly as a result. The two most common colors seen in America are cuckoo, a barred pattern, and black-copper.

Marans are tough and well suited to free ranging. They lay approximately 200 eggs per year and occasionally go broody.

Orpington

Orpingtons are an old English breed instantly recognizable for their big frames and fluffy feathers. They are one of the best backyard breeds as an overall blend of size, laying ability, and temperament. These gentle giants have deep bodies, short backs and enormous skirts of down.

Orpingtons are cold hardy and go broody often. Some lines have been bred to emphasize show value, while others still hold true to practicality. A good Orpington hen lays about 200 eggs per year and hatches out plenty of cockerels to fill the freezer. For a no-fuss, beautiful, and pleasant chicken, it's hard to overlook the Orpington.

Plymouth Rock

Plymouth Rocks are an American breed better known as the Barred Rock. They originated in the 19th century to be cold-hardy without sacrificing utility. The breeding plan was a success, and today Plymouth Rocks are some of the most common chickens in America. They are medium-sized and lay anywhere from 150 to 250 eggs per year.

This breed has been split along egg-laying and broiler lines. It is one of the contributors to the modern Cornish Rock hybrids that dominate the meat industry. Hatchery stock are selected for laying ability.

Rhode Island Red

This is the classic American chicken. They are a deep mahogany red and have long been prized as a dual-purpose bird. Unfortunately, that popularity has harmed the breed as a whole. Today, the typical hatchery Rhode Island Red tends to suffer from aggression and poor table qualities. If you can find a true, heritage Rhode Island Red, you will have a bird that is supremely self-sufficient, with an independent streak not marred by human aggression. A Red rooster is a fearsome protector of his flock, and this breed is even rumored to kill unwary foxes. Hens lay 200 to 250 eggs per year and are moderately broody.

Sussex

Another English Breed, Sussex were once a traditional table bird in England. They are built with long backs and deep bodies. The two most common colors seen in America are speckled, illustrated at the beginning of this section, and light, which features white feathers accentuated by black.

Sussex fill out quickly and lay medium, light-brown eggs. Hens manage anywhere from 200 to 250 eggs a year.

Wyandotte

Last but not least is the Wyandotte. These American chickens are another dual-purpose breed known for their amiable and relaxed temperaments. They have a distinctive poof of down along their backsides, which occasionally needs to be cleaned of debris and can cause fertility issues.

Hens lay about 200 eggs per year and are moderately broody. The most common colors are gold- and silver-laced, which look like eyeliner applied to the edges of feathers.

Chicken Housing

Chickens need adequate housing to protect them from the elements, most notably heat, cold, and drafts. Heat exhaustion and hypothermia kill in extreme cases, but even seemingly small things like poor ventilation will leave you with a sickly flock.

Chicken coops are designed to be airy and spacious. So long as certain requirements are met, there's no need to go out and buy an expensive pre-fabricated coop. It's far more affordable to construct your own or convert an old garden shed.

A chicken coop needs ventilation, roosts, nesting boxes, feeders, fountains, walls, and a roof. Everything else is optional. Each chicken should have at least four square feet of space in the coop and 10 square feet in a run.

Ventilation

Chickens produce a lot of poop. If you have never been around them before, you will be astonished at how often your birds squat down to relieve themselves. That's great for the garden, but it makes keeping the coop clean a challenge. Chicken feces breaks down and releases ammonia, which is dangerous at high levels. A coop that is inadequately ventilated will sting your eyes, smell of ammonia, and

116

burn any chickens forced to live in it. Because of this, a coop must have open ventilation at all times.

Ventilation keeps the coop dry in every season. More so than temperature, humidity determines flock health. A damp coop promotes frostbite, bacterial growth, and a number of other diseases and physical ailments.

Note that "ventilated" is not the same thing as "drafty." Drafts and dampness are the scourges of a chicken coop. Place ventilation above the level of the highest roosts, preferably along the roof. Plan at least one square foot of ventilation per chicken. These should remain open even in the winter, so long as they are not contributing to drafts.

Cover any open areas with durable hardware cloth and attach it firmly. Ventilation is the weakest point of the coop and the first place a predator will test. Animals like raccoons are stronger and more resourceful than they are given credit for, so use thick, sturdy wire that is too narrow for small hands to reach through and grab a chicken. All too often, flock owners have come out in the morning to find dead birds with their heads ripped off through otherwise secure wire. Any gap greater than ½" must be covered.

Roosts

Chickens in the wild take to the trees at night as protection against predators. Today, allowing domestic chickens to do the same would be a logistical nightmare, hence we confine them to coops. They still carry the instinct to sleep on branches, however, and are happiest when provided with a roost.

Most roosts are made from a narrow plank or wooden dowel. Metal becomes too cold in winter and should not be used. Planks offer more support and also keep chickens' feet warm. Some coops, especially converted sheds, have rafters that the chickens fly up into. Plan for at least one foot of roosting space per bird.

Below is a basic staggered roost:

Nesting Boxes

Hens like secure, quiet, and enclosed spaces to lay their eggs. By providing them with boxes to nest in, you also ensure that the majority of eggs can be collected from a single, centralized location in the morning.

Nesting boxes are very, very basic. Some people use old milk crates, others buy covered cat boxes. I prefer to use five gallon buckets as shown:

Young pullets should enter the boxes of their own accord, especially if they have older hens to watch. If a rebel decides to nest elsewhere, confine her to the coop for a few days and encourage her to use the box.

119

Once a habit is formed it is difficult to break.

Offer one nesting box for every five hens. They don't lay all at once, and there are often one or two "favorite" boxes that see most of the action.

Feeders and Fountains

Chickens need food and water. That's simple. The difficult part is keeping everything clean and free of gunk. Hang feeders and water fountains from the roof to discourage messy chickens from tracking shavings into them and knocking them over.

Runs vs. Free Ranging

The question of whether or not to free range elicits passionate opinions from backyard chicken owners. Free ranging gives chickens access to their natural food sources: plants, insects, and even small animals. They are able to roam about, dust bathe, and spread out as needed to maintain flock harmony.

On the other hand, free ranging inevitably leads to losses from predators. Sometimes a single chicken disappears, at other times the entire flock is wiped out in one afternoon. It is unpredictable and devastating. Coyotes, dogs, foxes, hawks, and bobcats are common predators, and they strike without warning.

If the risk is worth it, free ranging reduces feed

costs and produces better meat and eggs. Otherwise, your chickens will need a run.

Chicken Runs

Chicken runs are designed with two things in mind: keeping the chickens in and predators out. They must be strong and secure from above and below. String deer netting or hardware cloth over the top to deter hawks and also block chickens trying to flap their way to freedom. Light chickens can easily clear a six foot fence, but the heavy breeds usually can't muster the energy.

Old dog kennels make great chicken runs. They can be found used on local classifieds. The chain-link panels connect endlessly to expand as needed and, best of all, they are durable and cheap: two traits any homesteader should love. The downside is that they require flat ground to sit properly.

Small runs are also constructed from wooden frames with strong wire stretched between. These can be beautiful if done right but cost much more to complete.

The other common type of fencing is electric. Strands of high-tensile wire shock away predators and the chickens quickly learn to avoid them. This works best with large flocks that need substantial pasturage or smaller flocks kept on several acres. sustainably

Running Electricity

Electricity provides lighting and advanced ventilation in a coop. It is also a fire hazard if installed improperly or damaged.

Hens slow production in winter as light levels diminish as part of a natural resting period for their bodies. Artificial lights stimulate continuous laying, though perhaps at the expense of the birds' longevity.

Do not use heaters in the winter. They are too much of a risk, and a substantial difference in temperature between coop and run may kill birds. So long as your coop is dry and draft-free, your chickens should be able to handle freezing temperatures with little discomfort, courtesy of their feathers and mutual body heat.

Feeding Laying Chickens

Chickens are omnivores and, like all livestock, have their own unique diets. Because hens go through a rigorous physical process almost every day, and because so much can go wrong as it happens, nutrition is particularly important for layers.

Protein by Age for Layers

Young chicks, from zero to eight weeks old, are fed a high-protein starter formula that averages about 20 percent protein. They are then switched over to a grower formula at 17 or 18 percent until they reach point-of-lay, when the standard 16 percent layer formula is used. Protein levels dictate the growth of the bird. A broiler, for example, is fed more protein to pack on weight early. Layers grow slowly to promote a sound structure more conducive to egg production.

Feed Sources

A bag of chicken feed covers most, if not all, of your flock's dietary needs. Everything else picked up through scavenging is extra. Feed costs are projected to rise as of 2012, thanks in part to widespread drought in the United States. It is cheaper to buy in bulk or even mix your own feed at a feed mill. Also pick up some oyster shells as a protein supplement.

Feeding Chicks

Chicks eat only crumbles for the first few weeks. It's tempting to give them treats while they are still cute, but limit yourself to fluids like plain yogurt. Once they are a bit older, supply grit before adding solid treats to the menu. The chicks will know what to do with the grit and ingest as much as they need. Grit would be picked up naturally if they were raised outdoors and is used to grind up food.

You must decide whether to give medicated crumbles. These feeds contain antibiotics that protect chicks from Coccidiosis, a treatable but sometimes devastating disease of young birds. Those who would rather avoid the use of antibiotics can place some dirt from around the yard in the brooder, giving chicks time to build up their immunity as they would in the wild. Medicated feed is only necessary for those who have had severe Coccidiosis troubles before.

From then on, chickens can eat just about anything. They love dried mealworms, black oil sunflower seeds, and any scraps from the kitchen. They even relish eggs and chicken, but don't give them whole eggs lest you find yourself with an egg-picking problem. Leftover milk is another favorite and a good way to use up souring excess, though some believe it causes gastrointestinal upset. A mash of milk and feed, when served fresh, aids digestion and nutrient absorption.

Things to Avoid

Avoid giving chickens too much fat, including red meats. They cannot handle such dense energy and it eventually overwhelms the liver. Chickens can and will catch, kill, and eat small animals such as mice. This should be discouraged for sanitary reasons but is usually harmless.

Some foods to avoid:

- Avocados
- Citrus
- Pumpkin seeds
- Rhubarb
- Corn in large quantities
- Potatoes

Be aware that anything with a strong flavor manifests itself in the eggs. This causes many owners to withhold foods such as garlic and onions.

Some plants are also toxic to chickens, including many garden flowers and shrubs. If given the choice, however, chickens tend to overlook these bitter plants in favor of more palatable greenery.

Raising Chicks

So, you've picked out the right breed(s) for your farm and have everything set up for the new arrivals. You've found a hatchery with your chicks in stock, or perhaps you have picked them up from a local farm supply store or owner. Now what?

Getting chickens through their juvenile period is the most difficult part of raising them. Chicks are fragile, prone to a number of diseases and problems, and still learning how to do basic things like not drown in the water fountain. They need a special housing setup all their own.

Brooders

Chicks, when raised by their mother, stay underneath her downy skirts for warmth and protection. When raised by humans, however, another solution must be found. That is why chicks are isolated in a small enclosure called a brooder for several months. Brooders can be as simple as a tote from the store or as complex as a large hutch. What matters most is that the chicks have at least two square feet per bird, heat lamps, and plenty of food and water.

Heat lamps are the large red bulbs used in reptile tanks and sold at most hardware stores. They must be securely clamped into place to prevent a stray flyer knocking them over into the shavings. Place it in one corner of the brooder so that chicks can position themselves along a temperature gradient. Newborn chicks need about 100 degrees Fahrenheit; subtract another five degrees for every week thereafter. Following that progression, most chickens are able to handle room temperatures at six or seven weeks of age.

Brooders must be free of drafts. If a cold wind is bad for adults, it's even more devastating for young birds still incapable of regulating their own temperatures. Use shavings for bedding. Some claim that chicks eat them, mistaking them for food, but the larger flakes are too big for a chick and taste much worse than crumbles. Never use newspaper or a similar flat bedding. If a chick loses its footing on such a surface it can develop splayed leg, where the still-forming bones slide out of place and render it unable to walk until treated.

Chicks typically stay in the brooder until they are 10 to 12 weeks old. If there are no other chickens in the coop and temperatures are high enough, pullets and cockerels can be moved outside as early as eight weeks.

Integrating New Chicks

When integrating into an established flock, wait until the chicks are 12 weeks old or half their adult size. Adults are mercilessly territorial and do not appreciate the sudden appearance of intruders. Allow the two flocks to see each other through a barrier for at least a week before merging them. There will be some bullying, but do not remove any chicks unless blood is drawn. It might take a month or more for peace to reign once again, but it's all part of normal chicken behavior and should subside eventually.

Raising Chickens for Eggs

The majority of backyard flock owners keep chickens for their eggs. As a reliable source of protein that does not require slaughtering an animal, they are a staple of farm breakfasts and baking.

Once pullets reach laying age, around 20 weeks, they will naturally begin to produce eggs and seek out a laying spot. You will know they are nearing their first egg when they begin to crouch down for you or a rooster. In these situations, it's polite to give the pullet a good back scratch for her courtesy.

The majority of girls have no trouble making the transition, but some develop reproductive problems that plague them for the rest of their lives. Pullets start out laying small and sometimes deformed eggs and mature into their full potential over the course of a few months.

Hens lay in the mornings. If you hear a song of squawks coming from the coop at the crack of dawn, there are probably one or more ladies in the nesting boxes.

Common Health Problems

If all goes well, your chickens will lay without incident hundreds of times a year. Unfortunately, with so many opportunities for something to go wrong, it always happens at some point. Some reproductive issues are treatable, but most are ultimately fatal.

The most common egg-related trouble is binding. This occurs when an egg gets wedged in the cloaca or even further up the reproductive tract, backing up the hen's entire system and causing death within a few days. Symptoms include difficulty walking, straining, spending more time in the nesting box, and a downward-pointing tail. The hen's rear end swells as the situation worsens.

This can be alleviated by feeding the hen olive oil and massaging the vent area with Vaseline. Sometimes it works, sometimes it doesn't. A hen that binds once is likely to do it again.

Egg-yolk peritonitis is a more serious condition. This occurs when an egg yolk misses the duct that takes it to be enclosed in the shell and instead falls into the abdomen. There, the yolk feeds native bacteria, sparking a massive infection that quickly overwhelms a bird's system. Its most distinctive symptoms are a swollen abdomen and fever. If caught quickly, aggressive antibiotics may be able to save the hen. Like binding, a chicken that survives peritonitis is in greater danger of contracting it again.

There are also infectious diseases and scores of other problems, which I discuss at greater length in *Treating the Sick or Injured Chicken*. Although covering all of them would be too long for this section, watch chickens for signs of lethargy; a lack of interest in food or water; ruffled feathers; parasites; discharge from the eyes or beak; and visible injuries.

Broodiness

Sometimes, a hen decides that it's time to gather a clutch of eggs, hatch them, and raise herself some chicks. When this instinct is triggered, she becomes obsessed with sitting on eggs and will continue to brood even when they are taken from her.

A broody hen should either be given fertile eggs or have her resolve broken. During the brooding phase, she rarely leaves the nest for food or water and shuts down egg production entirely. If her eggs fail to hatch, she may continue brooding for weeks afterward.

To break a broody hen, cut her off from the nesting box. Toss her outside, close the coop doors and force her to sleep on the roost. Some broodies are more stubborn than others. It may take a while.

How Many Hens Per Person?

A dual-purpose hen in her prime lays about five eggs a week. How many hens your family needs depends on your egg consumption. Say, for example, that a family of four eats 50 eggs a week through breakfasts and baking. That family needs 10 hens, with a few more to cover losses and the eventual decline in productivity.

Track your egg usage throughout a month to get a ballpark number. Chicken owners tend to end up drowning in eggs, but there are always neighbors happy to take the extras.

The Issue of Roosters

To clear up a few common myths: Hens do not need a rooster to lay eggs, and fertilized eggs collected within a few days will not crack open to reveal a partially formed chick. Fertilized eggs do not taste any different from regular eggs. The average flock of laying hens gets by just fine without roosters, who tend to be aggressive and somewhat rapacious.

On the other hand, roosters make it possible to hatch out new generations, watch over their ladies fiercely, and help them find food and get to safety. The ratio of hens to roosters should be 7:1 or higher.

Chicks that are straight run, meaning they haven't been sexed, begin to show sexual differences beginning at three weeks. Extra cockerels can be given away (most people won't buy them for much) or raised for the table.

LIVESTOCK I

Livestock come both large and small. The big animals produce more in quantity, but they also take up greater space and resources. The chicken is a relatively small bird. To get started with mammals, I recommend a creature of similar stature.

Rabbits are no longer thought of as a meat animal in America, having gradually become pets and cartoon characters. Their original purpose, though, was as a fast-growing source of lean, nutritious meat. A doe kept on a conservative breeding schedule bears about 50 kits per year, which are mature and ready to butcher by 10 weeks.

I like rabbits so much that I raise them even with a mild allergy to their fur. They are a great gateway mammal for larger livestock, teaching the basics of reproduction and butchering, and are at the same time one of the best meat animals you will ever own.

Rabbit Breeds

Nowadays, most rabbits are bred for pet and show qualities instead of meat, but a few strains are still selected for their qualities as livestock.

Californians

Californians were developed in the early 20th century as a hybrid of the New Zealand White and a few other breeds. They are a vigorous, meaty rabbit with soft pelts. Expect a five-pound fryer in 10 weeks from good meat lines.

New Zealand Whites

New Zealand Whites are the meat rabbit of choice. Despite their name, they are an American breed. They have a feed conversion ratio of approximately 4:1 and are undemanding to keep. There are also New Zealand Reds, if you prefer a colored rabbit.

Rabbit Housing

Rabbits are kept in hutches, which must be sturdy and well-ventilated in both winter and summer. Larger breeding operations use hanging cages, but I only recommend them if the floor is covered to protect the rabbits' feet. Hutches are usually wooden and supported on legs to keep them out of reach of predators. They are simple to build but also available online or in some stores.

Plan to have at least four square feet per rabbit. Does that are not pregnant can be housed together but must have their own space as mothers. Bucks are kept alone and only interact with does to breed. For a small set-up of one buck and two does, that means three hutches.

Rabbits are especially vulnerable to heat and should not be kept in full sunlight. Prevent access to treated wood surfaces, for they love to chew, and protect them from precipitation with a solid roof. Use hardware cloth or another strong mesh to line open areas. Provide as much ventilation as possible.

Line the floor with straw, hay, or pine shavings and provide something for the rabbits to chew. The downside to hutches is that they must be cleaned out regularly, whereas cages allow most urine and droppings to pass through to a pan below. A long, narrow design makes it easier to scoop out waste materials.

Rabbits deteriorate quickly at temperatures higher than 80 degrees. Always be mindful of temperatures within the hutch and work fast to keep rabbits cool. Freeze water bottles, treats, and towels and place them inside the hutch for the rabbits to enjoy. Situate a fan near the opening of a hutch to circulate air. If the rabbits are still stretched out and panting, bring them into an air conditioned area until they recover.

Rabbits are hardier in the cold and tolerate most temperatures when given adequate bedding and a draft-free sleeping area. Cover the hutch at night with a tarp if you are worried. I have heard of some owners giving their rabbits hot water bottles to sleep on at night.

Feeding Rabbits

Rabbits are herbivores with a staple diet of grass hay and protein-rich pellets. They love just about any other green, as well; vegetables and fruits are almost all acceptable, but avoid iceberg lettuce, which is nutritionally useless and too watery, and don't feed them many sweets.

If you are looking for a more sustainable solution, it is of course possible to raise rabbits on a natural diet of non-toxic plants. Gardeners find a welcome ally in their rabbits, which are happy to dispose of picked weeds. Fresh-grown alfalfa is also an excellent supplement. This is one of those subjects that I wish I could cover in greater detail but, unfortunately, changes with every zip code. Identify and check everything before you toss it into the hutch.

A small enclosure also allows rabbits to graze freely over a patch of grass. Again, I have found chain-link panels to be a portable and inexpensive solution.

Raising Rabbits

A doe can be healthily bred six times a year. Four or five litters are easier on her system. Bring the doe to the buck's hutch when you're ready to breed. They do not have regular 'heat' periods and become fertile as soon as they are mounted. Breed meat rabbits once the does are near adult size, at about six months. The buck mounts the doe and falls off when he is done. Breed again in five or six hours.

Gestation takes 31 days. The doe begins building her nest and pulling fur as her time nears. If everything goes well, she will deliver a healthy litter. Check them over for any dead kits and remove as needed. Make sure they are warm before leaving them to their mother's care.

The average litter consists of eight kits, though a single doe can have as much as 20 at a time. Meat rabbits are slaughtered between eight and 10 weeks of age. This is due to practicality – does hit puberty at around eight weeks and growth drops off sharply at 10.

Dispatch a rabbit by breaking its neck or delivering a sharp blow to the skull. To break the neck, stretch the rabbit out and then pull its head up and back in a sharp, sustained motion until you feel it snap. Then remove the head and forelegs with a knife and hang the body by the hind legs to bleed out.

Skin the rabbit by cutting the pelt between and around the legs, then rolling it down over the shoulders. It should come off like a sweater. Cut the belly open carefully from genitals to chest, being careful not to puncture any organs. At this point, scissors come in handy. Cut the pelvis for easier access and scoop out the guts. Remove the back feet at the joint to finish the process. Rabbits can be cooked whole or chopped into smaller pieces. Use the meat like you would chicken.

If you have never killed anything before, steel yourself and just do it. The more indecisive you are the more likely the animal is to suffer. Once the dying is over, the rest is easy.

How Many Rabbits?

Start with three rabbits, two does and a buck, unless you know you enjoy rabbit meat and can handle raising and slaughtering waves upon waves of bunnies. Two healthy does can birth at least 80 young fryers per year, or about 150 pounds of dressed-weight meat. From personal experience, three rabbits combined with other livestock are enough for two adults, but they require fresh blood periodically to maintain genetic strength.

Breeding does on a rotation schedule will give you plenty of fresh meat year-round. Figure that one fryer can feed two people.

WATER STORAGE

Water consumption is a major, if unheralded, problem for the United States and the larger world. Besides the droughts that continue to ruin farmers across America, there is the issue of pollution and waste facilitated by almost every household seeping into our drinking supply.

An entire farm can wither away in just a few weeks without water, including its residents. Knowing how to collect, store, and purify water is essential not only from an environmental standpoint, but also as part of a basic preparedness plan. Do not rely on electricity to give you safe drinking water.

Estimate one gallon of water per person per day. Most will go to drinking, with a bit left over for a quick wash. Livestock and crops require more, to the point that storing water for them is unrealistic. That is why it is so important to secure a sustainable water source.

Securing a Source of Water

The three main types of water for collection purposes come from underground, the surface, and the sky. All three should be part of your survival plans.

Ground Water

Most rural homes get their water from a well. If your property doesn't have one, dig it. If you do have one, install a manual pump. Groundwater is the purest water to be found, assuming agricultural chemicals have traveled down to its level. It's also the most reliable source, and a good well can last for decades of continuous use. A manual pump guarantees access to that water even during an emergency power outage. Farmers traditionally pumped well-water with a windmill.

Rain Water

Rain is the second purest type of water, but it may contain acid as well as pollutants picked up from the air. It is not recommended for potable use unless filtered thoroughly beforehand, but pH-neutral water is fine for plants and livestock. Collect rain water by installing metal gutters and rain barrels.

Surface Water

Surface water is a last resort. It can contain

harmful bacteria, parasites, and any number of chemicals, particularly if it is stagnant. It's also difficult to collect and must be hauled. If a property is far from any source of water, it quickly becomes a long and irksome chore.

Storing Water

Keep water in a sterile plastic container. A 55-gallon barrel is the common choice. Scrub and disinfect any container thoroughly before filling with water, and never use anything that has held chemicals or gasoline. If using untreated water, add eight drops of bleach for every gallon. This kills organisms and makes it safe for human or animal consumption.

Water that sits for too long will have a strange taste to it due to a lack of oxygen. Sloshing the water between two containers helps to alleviate the flavor.

It's recommended that even bleached water be purified once more before drinking, especially if it came from rain or surface water. Be safe! We have become accustomed to taking safe water for granted, but things can go wrong very fast in the molecule that makes life possible.

Purifying Water

When drinking harvested water, do everything in your power to eliminate parasites such as Giardia. There are numerous ways to purify water, including using bleach as mentioned in the last section. The easiest method, though, is to boil it.

Some tablets, like iodine or chlorine dioxide, are not always effective against parasites and should only be used in conjunction with boiling.

Bring water to a vigorous boil for one full minute to make it potable. It takes some time for the water to heat up and cool down again, meaning you may not get that sparkling glass of ice water, but this is the most secure way to kill any unfriendly organisms. There are solar-powered heaters on the market to purify water without electricity or a fire, or use a wood stove.

Perhaps a more convenient option is a gravity flow filter, which uses a string of chemical processes to filter water as it is pulled downward by gravity. These systems can filter many gallons a day with minimal effort on the part of the family. Ensure that any gravity filter you buy is guaranteed against micro-organisms.

ALTERNATIVE ENERGY I

Continuing the preparedness topics, there is also the matter of energy to consider. One of the main reasons people get into homesteading is for the peace of mind that comes from being able to survive without modern conveniences.

Alternative energy is any kind of energy not reliant on the electrical grid. Wind and solar power get the most attention, but they will not be part of this book until years four and five. In the meanwhile, you don't need to sit in the dark every time a storm blows through. Being ready with a generator and batteries should see a family through most disasters.

More importantly, start changing the way you think about electricity. From now on, pay attention to your energy consumption and find ways to lessen it in preparation for more drastic renovations later.

Developing a Backup System

Once the power goes out, there is no guarantee that it will come back any time soon. Generators allow you to gather information, preserve the food in your fridge, and run a few lights while you wait for the power company to swoop in to the rescue.

When used incorrectly, generators kill. Never run one indoors or within three feet of an opening into the house. Do not use a generator in the rain or other wet conditions. Be mindful of your own mental and physical condition around a generator. Signs of weakness or confusion mean it's time to walk away.

Most generators run on gasoline, which also needs to be stored safely. Keep gasoline in approved plastic containers well away from the house. Never light a flame near stored gas. Rotate it out once a year or more and leave room in the container for the gasoline to expand.

Check local ordinances for both generators and gasoline storage. Many towns and cities have laws governing when generators can be run and how gasoline can be kept. Above all, be safe. Remember that gasoline, and especially its vapor, is extremely flammable with an explosive power akin to dynamite. There's nothing worse than losing your property to a fire that could have been prevented.

Preparing for Life Without Power

When the lights go off, every family member should know what to do. Don't expect to learn how to fire up a generator in the dark. Have a flashlight with fresh batteries in every room to make navigation easier.

Short power outages are rarely a big deal. Once the novelty wears off the tedium sets in and it's a simple matter of waiting for the power company to do its job.

If you know that you will be waiting for more than one day, on the other hand, it's time to jump into action. A battery-powered or hand-cranked radio provides updates on road crews' status and local events. Start by assessing the safety conditions outdoors. If a large storm is currently ripping across the countryside, wait inside until it passes.

If there's no immediate danger, start the generator by following the device's instructions and choose which essentials need to be on. The fridge should be powered at least every six hours to preserve food, more for a freezer. Ration your gasoline according to the severity of the situation.

A supply of canned goods comes in handy during extensive outages, such as the deadly blizzards that occasionally leave thousands stranded for a week or more. You will also be able to tap into your water reserves to drink, flush the toilets, shower, and care for your property.

It is possible to survive by huddling in the dark, but it is not efficient, fun, or economical. By spending a few hours preparing ahead of time, your family can weather any loss of power with minimal inconvenience and emerge unscathed.

Cutting Energy Consumption

Part of living more responsibly means staying mindful of your lifestyle and how even the smallest actions can build up to huge consequences. Energy use is one of the most important areas to apply this philosophy.

Start with the basics, like consciously turning off lights in empty rooms and going to bed earlier. Take showers, not baths Install environmentally friendly appliances during renovations or, even better, start doing things by hand rather than relying on machines. Turn up the thermostat in summer and turn it back down in winter.

Not only will this free up some cash to invest in your homestead, it will also improve your environmental impact and make it easier to adjust to alternative energy in the future.

YEAR THREE

GARDENING III

In year two, you expanded your garden significantly and learned about the process of fertilizing soils. This year focuses on establishing infrastructure to prolong your growing season and offer greater control over the soil.

The vegetables added are, with a few exceptions, optional, and they tend to require a little more work to cultivate and prepare successfully. They reward the faithful with distinctive flavors and plentiful harvests.

Don't be afraid to experiment with what you like and don't like. At this point you should have a good understanding of how much your family eats of each vegetable. Estimates of plants per person are still provided, but in the end a family's garden is a uniquely personal affair. There is no one size fits all.

New Vegetables

Artichokes

Artichokes are a variety of thistle with large, edible bulbs. They prefer mild climates with warm, wet summers and cool winters but can be grown as annuals in Zones 7 and colder. They are rarely sown from seed and are instead purchased as immature split roots.

Perennials need six foot spacing but annuals get by with four. Artichokes benefit from frequent fertilizing and watering. Side dress them every month.

Perennials put up two harvests a year in optimal growing conditions. Cut the stalks off at the ground after each harvest to promote new growth. The artichokes are ready to collect when they are large, fleshy, and still tight-packed.

Square feet per plant: 16

Plants per person: 2

Asparagus

Asparagus is one of the few perennial vegetables and takes years to get going, but it is also well worth the wait. It is one of the most balanced vegetables available from a nutritional standpoint. As a perennial, it needs a dormant period and cold winters to survive.

Asparagus is grown from "crowns," which look like, and are, straggly lumps of roots. Dig trenches 6" deep and space the crowns 12" apart. Cover the crowns with three inches of soil until they have sprouted ferns, and then fill in the rest of the hole.

Asparagus performs best in raised beds. During the first year, do not harvest any shoots that emerge. They spread into ferns, which strengthen the crown and provide a stronger first harvest. You can begin cutting spears in the second year, but it is advisable to wait until the third or fourth. Once established, asparagus plants are relatively hardy but need an annual fertilization to maintain peak output.

Harvest spears until June, at which point the plant should be allowed to fern. Cut spears at ground level, and only remove ferns when they are dead and brown.

Square feet per plant: 1

Plants per person: 15

Cabbages

Cabbages are an excellent crop, if not very exciting. They are easy to recognize by their large, leafy heads and store well over winter.

Sow cabbage seeds outdoors in early spring and late summer. There are different varieties depending on your desired growing season. Thin the seedlings out to at least 12" spacing, but more is better. Cabbages are no-fuss. They are not fond of heat, so keep them well-watered in the summer months. If your soil is nutritious and you keep the bugs away from them, they grow without complaint.

Harvest when the heads are at your preferred size, before they split open.

Square feet per plant: 2.25

Plants per person: 10

Celery

Celery is a difficult plant to grow. In fact, it may be the most challenging of all vegetables. It only operates within a narrow temperature range and requires special attention throughout the growing season. There are two main varieties of celery: stalk and cutting. Stalk celery is what is found in the grocery store, while cutting celery is more cold-tolerant and produces shorter, smaller stalks with bushy foliage.

Start seeds indoors and do not transplant until the daily low temperature exceeds 50 degrees. Temperatures above 75 degrees also harm the plant. Transplant them with 12" spacing in a bed that holds water well and contains plenty of organic materials. Fertilize regularly and don't let these plants run out of water.

Celery shoots up multiple stalks. Harvest as soon as they reach an acceptable size, about 16 weeks, by cutting them near the base. The darker the stalk, the more nutritious it is, though it may also be tougher.

Square feet per plant: 1

Plants per person: 5

Herbs

Although not technically a vegetable, herbs are what make meals stand out. They were a valuable commodity in ancient times as a way to liven up diets full of staid beef, chicken, and cabbage. Today, they are still an essential part of most recipes.

Growing herbs is easy. Many families keep a few potted plantings on the porch for quick access. They are eaten fresh or chipped and dried for later use. Some of the most popular herbs include basil, oregano, dill, rosemary, chives, parsley, savory, and thyme. If you plan to use them often, populate a 100-square-foot bed.

Herbs are grown like standard vegetables. Start them indoors or after the last frost date, keep them watered, and they will flourish. Harvest adult-sized leaves. The drying process is covered later on in the canning and preserving section.

Square feet per plant: 1

Plants per person: 10 or more

Hot Peppers

Bell peppers were introduced in year one, but now it's time to add some kick to your garden. Like herbs, peppers are beloved for their ability to spice up any dish. The burning sensation caused by hot peppers causes an effect similar to the rush after exercising.

The most common chile peppers grown are jalapeños, poblanos, and cayenne. Some are only mildly spicy, while others are almost unbearable. They mature slowly but put on bountiful crops in mid to late summer.

Start peppers indoors. They take a week or two to germinate, so don't panic when everything else is up and the peppers are still barren. Plant them in a sunny spot with 18" spacing and fertilize about once a month if needed.

Peppers ripen at different times and in different ways, depending on type. As a general rule, green chiles are unripe, but still edible, and have the mildest flavors. They then become, orange, red, and even black, heat increasing with color. Cut the peppers from the plant with a sharp knife to avoid damaging the branches.

Square feet per plant: 2.25

Plants per person: 5

Parsnips

The parsnip is a vegetable perfectly suited to colder climates. When exposed to frost, this root develops a sweet, mellow flavor that is unbeatable when sautéed with butter.

Parsnips have doubtful fertility. Sow plenty of seeds in mid-spring and thin the sprouts to at least 6" spacing. Work the soil deeply before planting. Parsnips are harvested once they are 1" to 2" in diameter. Waiting a week or two after the frosts start improves flavor. An easy storage method is to cover them with mulch, let them overwinter, and dig them up before they develop new growth in January or February.

Square feet per plant: .5

Plants per person: 15

Squash

Squashes are sprawling, climbing vines that are simple to grow and offer a big return on investment. Summer squashes like zucchini and crookneck will overwhelm with your with their output. Winter squashes such as acorn and butternut are very nutritious and ripen while the rest of the garden is shutting down.

Plant summer squash in early spring and winter squash a couple months later. Soil should be rich and have a pH of 6.0 to 6.5. Build small mounds and grow three plants on each. Allow 50 square feet per mound.

Squashes spread out and begin developing gourds with little trouble for the gardener. Some side-dressed fertilizer and water are appreciated every once in a while, but most squashes grow without a hitch. Heavy rains or wet soil may cause rot along the fruits' undersides.

Summer squashes are ripe when they have reached a mature size and weight but are still somewhat tender to the touch. They should be eaten fresh. Winter squashes take longer to mature because they must be left on the vine until their skin is too hard to dent with a fingernail. This is what lets them be stored for months at a time.

Square feet per plant: 16

Plants per person: 6

Soil Amendment II

In year two, this book covered how to discover and improve the nutritional qualities of your soil. The other factor in plant performance, as far as dirt goes, is acidity. Most plants do well in a neutral soil, but others prefer greater alkalinity or acidity. A difference of one point is not as small as it sounds: A 6.0 pH sample is ten times more acidic than a 7.0.

Your local extension office should have an affordable pH kit or testing service. Another option is to grab some soil and place it in two separate containers. Pour vinegar into one and a solution of baking soda into the other. If there's a reaction to the vinegar (bubbling), then the soil is alkaline, and a similar reaction to the baking soda points to acidic. This doesn't tell you the exact pH, but it provides an easy starting point to amending.

Increasing Alkalinity

Acidic soil is amended with lime to increase the pH. The amount needed to raise the garden to a 6.5 depends on the starting pH and the earth's composition. Sandy soils need less, clay needs more. To boost the pH of good loam by 1.0, plan to use about 16 pounds of limestone per 100 square feet.[14]

Increasing Acidity

Soil that is too alkaline, or above 7.5 pH, is just as damaging. Lower pH with a variety of materials. Peat moss is a common choice, but pine needles can also be mixed into the soil as a cheap fix. Sulfur is the most popular solution. Two pounds per 100 square feet should lower the pH by about 1.0[14] but, again, always follow labeled instructions or recommendations.

Raised Beds and Hoop-Houses

In the first two years, I advised you to divide your garden into wide strips with grass walkways between the rows. This was partially to make management efficient, but it was also setting the groundwork for building raised beds and hoop-houses.

Raised Beds

Raised beds are becoming more and more popular. Gardeners are able to control exactly what goes into their soil, which also drains better and wastes less fertilizer. Plants can be grouped closer together while still growing more produce.

One important thing to note with raised beds is that, though you will still save space, the plants need to be slightly further apart to accommodate the loss of rows (planting in a grid as opposed to a line.) For example, parsnips can be placed as close as 4" together so long as the rows are at least 18" apart, but in a raised bed they need to be about 8" apart. This is still less cultivated space overall, but it's something to keep in mind with each plant.

Rotate beds every year to prevent the build-up of diseases and pests, and remember that they need to be watered more often.

Construction of a Raised Bed

Don't spend a fortune on raised beds. So long as the lumber is untreated, any wood will do. Scavenge pallets from local businesses and check classified listings for unwanted planks, but even new lumber is not particularly expensive. Concrete blocks also work well for raised beds. Don't buy a kit:, since they are very easy to make.

Three 8' x 4" x 6" planks yield a 32-square-foot bed. Four feet is a good width to still reach the middle, and the bed can be extended as long as needed. Post stakes at the corner and sporadically along the length for support. Scrape the ground level and remove sod, though the latter is not strictly necessary. Then nail or screw the boards into place.

Fill the bed with a mix of top-soil, humus, compost, and some fertilizer to begin with. Later soil tests will fine-tune the blend, but for the first year it's hard to go wrong with moderation. Once the dirt is in and any manure has had time to decompose, the bed is ready for planting. Construct as many as needed in orderly rows with walkways in between.

Hoop-Houses

Hoop-houses are simply large, more affordable greenhouses. They are usually open-ended arches covered in clear plastic sheeting that stretch across a raised garden bed, as shown:

Hoop-houses regulate temperatures in all seasons but are primarily used in the early spring and late fall. In milder climates, vegetables can be grown all year under a hoop-house, but even areas that see rough winters can extend their growing season by weeks or months. With hoop-houses, seedlings are transplanted earlier and mature plants survive longer. Not every bed needs a hoop-house. Save them for the plants with the longest growing seasons and cold-hardy vegetables that may be able to make it through the winter with some assistance.

Construction of a Hoop-House

A hoop-house designed for a standard vegetable bed has three basic components: hoops, plastic, and support. PVC pipe is the preferred material for both the hoops and the support. A 10-foot long, 1/2-inch thick pipe is sturdy but flexible enough to bend as needed. Use ¾-inch pipes buried into the dirt to hold them on either side of the bed. The ¾-inch pipes should be 12 inches long with at least four inches sticking out of the ground. Another PVC pipe running along the top and zip-tied into place will help keep the whole thing aligned properly, but if the supports are implemented properly everything should stay put.

Next, stretch a clear, visqueen-like plastic over the PVC skeleton. Weigh it down on the edges with wooden planks, bricks, or clamps. The plastic can be removed on sunny days.

When compared to the increased produce they provide, the low cost of each bed and hoop-house is well worth the investment. Expect to spend approximately $50 for a 64 square foot bed, but that can be reduced even further with some creative bargaining and salvaging. With hoop-houses installed, the need for an actual greenhouse is greatly reduced.

LIVESTOCK II

Chickens and rabbits are the perfect beginner's livestock, but they can't do everything. For a source of milk and red meat, there is nothing easier than the goat. Female goats are does, males are bucks, juveniles are kids, and neutered males are wethers.

Goats are ruminants, like cows, and have in fact been domesticated longer than their larger counterparts. They take up less space, consume less feed, are safer to handle, and can still provide more than enough meat and dairy for the average family.

There is a stigma in much of the United States surrounding eating or drinking the byproducts of goats. These creatures have a reputation for eating anything, and there is an old myth that their milk tastes 'goaty.' Not to mention the fact that the average American is locked into the idea of 'right' food and 'strange' food.

If raised and housed properly, goat's milk tastes almost identical to cow's and is better for digestion. Smaller fat globules mean that it is naturally homogenized and may not cause a reaction in those who are dairy-intolerant.

Dairy goats are bred to produce copious amounts of milk, while meat goats are selected to put on muscle quickly. This year focuses on dairy breeds.

Taking on goats brings more responsibilities. Does in milk must be tended to twice a day. They are also not so easily replaced as chickens, meaning more money will be spent on veterinary costs to keep them healthy and sound.

Common Dairy Goat Breeds

There are a number of dairy breeds found in the United States. The milk estimates in this section are averages and vary wildly based on line quality. A top dairy doe can give over 5,000 pounds of milk in a 300-day lactating period, but a poor one may only scrape together a few hundred.

Alpine

Alpines are a French breed known for being reliable milkers that give birth to meaty bucks. They are large, friendly, and intelligent. Mature does give an average of 2,266 pounds of milk per year. Alpine milk contains an average of 3.4 percent butterfat.[15]

Nigerian Dwarf

The Nigerian Dwarf is, at its name implies, the smallest dairy goat. Where other breeds stand 30 inches or more at the shoulder, the Nigerian doe stands at a mere 18. Their diminutive stature and 6 percent butterfat milk makes them popular among small farmers and cheese-makers alike. A typical Nigerian gives 900 pounds of milk a year.[16]

Nubian

Nubians are easy to pick out thanks to their Roman noses and long, floppy ears. They produce less milk than some other dairy breeds, at around 1,820 pounds per year, but make up for it with 4.9 percent butterfat, second only to Nigerians.[15]

LaMancha

LaManchas hail from Oregon and bear the distinctive trait of having almost no ears. Their hearing is unimpaired, but the cartilage and skin has been whittled away through years of selective breeding. Today the LaMancha is one of America's favorite dairy goats. A good doe will give approximately 2,100 pounds of milk per year at 3.2 percent butterfat.[15]

Oberhasli

Oberhasli are one of the oldest dairy goat breeds but still rare in America. They are prolific milkers, producing about 2,146 gallons a year with a butterfat content around 3.9 percent.[15] Oberhasli are vigorous, hardy goats and do well in colder climates.

Saanen

Saanens are the largest dairy goats with does standing an average of 32 inches tall at the shoulder. They are a regal breed, producing approximately 2,577 pounds per year with 3.3 percent butterfat.[15]

Toggenburg

Finally, Toggenburgs are a medium-sized breed with a stocky build. They are known for their finely shaped and attached udders, and perform well for their size at about 2,115 pounds a year at 3.2 percent butterfat.[15]

Making a Choice

Each breed has its own advantages and disadvantages, and the flavor of milk also differs between them. Before making a commitment, spend some time with your breed of choice to make sure that they are right for your family.

Don't be afraid to look at hybrids. These crosses between dairy or even meat breeds often have improved milk production and sturdier constitutions than their purebred parents.

Goat Housing

Goats are hardy animals, but they need some protection from the elements and are clever escape artists. In order to keep them safe from nature and themselves, you must provide vigorous fencing and shelter from the wind, rain, and snow.

Goat Shelters

Large goat operations use full barns to house their stock, but a homestead is not so demanding. As herd animals, goats prefer "open" housing, which allows them to mingle freely and does not confine them to stalls. A simple shed is often sufficient. Aim for at least 10 square feet per goat. The roomier the housing the less stressed your goats will be. Focus on ventilation; goats don't react well to humidity.

Besides some walls and a roof, goats need a feed trough, water, a milking station, and a kidding pen. A milking station is a clean, clear spot where goats can be tethered, either by halter or by stanchion. A kidding pen is a secure area where does can safely give birth in privacy.

Goats are not picky creatures. If you value a picture-perfect farm, you can opt for a miniature red barn and white picket fence, or you can save yourself a lot of time and money. Pallets, again, are an excellent source of cheap or free lumber.

Few drafts make few problems. Thick plywood or a sheet of tin are good, wind-resistant materials for walls. Dig in four sturdy posts for support, construct a roof, and add a door. Goats push, pull, and climb, so make sure everything can handle the attentions of a 150-pound animal.

Use straw or wood shavings as bedding. It should be thick enough to provide a comfortable cushion and cleaned regularly. Before winter, add additional bedding to hold warmth on cold nights.

For more advanced ideas, Carol Ekarius' "How to Build Animal Housing" has blueprints for nearly every type of livestock and comes highly recommended.

Goat Fencing

Goats can be kept in the same yard or pasture as chickens, sheep, cows, and most other farm animals. They are highly intelligent and have a tendency to covet the forbidden. That means they like to scramble, dig, and squeeze their way out of vulnerable fencing.

Any enclosure should be at least four feet high: Six is preferable. The chain link panels mentioned in year two for chicken runs work well with goats, too, and the two species make for amiable companions. Goats cannot, however, have access to the chicken feed. Plan to have at least 30 square feet of run per goat.

More conventional fencing includes woven wire and electric. Woven wire is the standard gridwork of metal wire used for goats, sheep, cows, and horses. It must be smaller than 4" x 4" to prevent the goats getting their heads stuck. Electric fencing is better for the stubborn troublemakers who insist on breaking out. After a few zaps it instills a mental barrier just as effective as any physical one. A six-string fence of high-tensile wire also keeps out most predators. Consider running two strands of electric over the top and along the middle of a woven wire fence for extra protection.

Lush ground supports about five goats per acre or eight or more with rotation.

Feeding Goats

Goats, like cows, are ruminants. They have a specialized digestive tract stretched over four stomach chambers meant to wring every last scrap of nutrients from grasses and plants other animals would starve on. They will eat everything from bark to brambles to poison ivy and thrive on it.

Unlike cows, goats do not spend most of their time grazing. They prefer dense, woody lands with plenty of shrubs and trees to nibble. Because of their complementary grazing styles, goats are often pastured with or ahead of sheep. The former level the pasture to grass while the latter act as lawnmowers. The only things to keep in mind are that goats need more copper in their diets, tend to dominate the sheep, and are just close enough genetically to occasionally interbreed. Goats also pasture well with cattle.

A diet of hay with grain is necessary for animals kept on smaller pastures and in the winter. Supplement with a mineral mix or blocks that the goats can access as they please. Legume hays are paired with fewer grains, and grass hay is fed with more to provide a proper balance of proteins. A doe in milk is given plenty of hay and 1 ½ to 3 pounds of grain per day, give or take. Feed twice a day.

Goats rely on bacteria in their gut to break down foods. Those bacteria exist in certain quantities depending on the goat's typical diet. Changing feeds or adding something new too quickly causes bloat- a catastrophic buildup of gases that, in worst-case scenarios, can stop the heart and lungs. Always introduce new foods gradually to give a goat's rumen a chance to adjust.

Buying Goats

Any goats you purchase will be around for years to come, so it's important to choose well the first time. Once you've narrowed down a list of possible breeds, check their national associations' webpages for a list of registered breeders. They have some of the best stock to start with.

You can also check the local farm listings on websites like Craigslist, or attend livestock auctions. Animals purchased through these venues are at greater risk of carrying disease and inferior genes, but it is possible to find real bargains.

While you are relatively inexperienced, it is better to spend a little extra and go through a breeder with an established reputation for producing fine, healthy animals that give generous milk. Most goat breeders are helpful, dedicated, and may become a lasting source of advice for years to come.

When beginning with goats, there are arguments to be made for buying both kids and adults. Kids are cute and give you time to learn the ropes of owning a goat before worrying about milking and reproduction. Adult does start providing milk sooner, if not immediately, and already know the basics of being handled by humans.

Whichever you choose, go into the buying process with a clear idea of what to look for, both good and bad.

Weanlings are difficult to judge for expert and beginner alike. They are all knobbly knees and odd tufts of hair, and they rarely sit still long enough to look them over properly. This makes them a risk: It's hard to know how a goat kid will turn out.

When buying kids, your best bet is to look to the parents and immediate family. Start by examining the mother. A dairy doe should be sturdy, yet refined, with fine bones and good carriage. She should have a wide stomach, large nostrils, and a strong jaw. When viewed from above, she resembles a wedge tapering at the shoulders. The topline is straight, and the stomach slopes gently downwards.

Her udder should be attached high and tight to the body, not low and sagging. The teats are well-placed and large enough to be gripped by hand, but not oversized. Don't be impressed by a huge udder: It doesn't indicate actual milk production, but a small udder should also be avoided. Bear in mind that does that have never kidded will have smaller udders.

Ask for milking records for a doe or her mother. If you can, milk her twice yourself, once in the morning and once that night, to get an honest assessment of her output. The milk should be free of strings, clumps, and blood and flow easily from each teat.

A good doe is sweet and gentle. Aggression is a bad sign and may carry through to the kids. Always be wary when buying kids without the mother present. A strong doe is a major selling point, the lack of one suggests weak genetics.

Also ask about the medical history of the goat and its family. Has she received a CDT vaccine? Is she on a regular worming schedule? Has she been bred before? Has her herd been tested for any diseases, and if so when? If a doe has been bred, get a service memo to confirm the breeding. Find out what the goats have been eating to make the transition more comfortable. The more information you get, the better off you'll be.

Transport goats in a livestock trailer or a large dog kennel. Some kids are docile enough to be driven home on a lap, but you are asking for trouble if one develops a rogue bounce in her posterior.

How Many Goats?

Goats are sociable animals, and they enjoy having company. By buying two does and rotating breedings, you should have milk the entire year. The number kept beyond that depends on the size of your family and typical milk consumption.

Assuming one doe produces a gallon of milk a day, and assuming she often has at least two kids to feed, a good estimate is one active doe for every member of the family. Later, if you choose to raise some hogs, an additional doe will provide them with plenty of fattening milk. Start with two or three and then expand as you see fit.

Keeping Bucks

Does are sweet, gentle creatures. Bucks are a different story. They cannot be kept near does in milk because they cause a "bucky" flavor and tend to harass the herd and the people caring for it. That means they need separate housing and a companion all their own.

Bucks are also, forgive the term, royal buttheads. During the breeding season they urinate on their own legs and faces, developing a powerful odor and acting generally horribly.

Because they are such a pain to live with, many

small farmers do not keep bucks. Instead, they rely on artificial insemination or stud services when it comes time to put the ladies in a family way. I recommend staying away from bucks until you are familiar with does and have been around males at their worst.

Caring For Goats

Give your new arrivals some time to explore their surroundings and keep their exposure to new foods limited for at least a week.

Once a year, give each goat a CDT vaccination and pneumonia vaccinations are recommended as well. Worm them at around the same time. Ivomec is safe for pregnant does. Goats need higher doses than most other livestock, so research each brand carefully before administering.

There is a "withholding" time after worming when milk is not deemed safe for human consumption. That is why most farmers worm their herds around month before the does give birth, during a natural dry spell.

Trim goat hooves once every three months or so. They grow just like fingernails and become awkward or even painful if left to their own devices. Trimming hooves is probably the most nerve-wracking task for new goat owners. Buy dedicated goat hoof trimmers online or from a farm supply store beforehand and set the goat up in her stanchion with a bucket of grain.

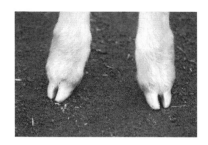

You are aiming for neat, compact hooves, like those of a young kid. Start by cleaning the hoof with a pick and a sterile rag. Work out all the debris and begin clipping. Think of it as sculpting the hoof. Take it slowly to begin with, and don't be too ambitious.

Try to find an experienced veterinarian or goat owner to teach you how to cut feet properly. If you can't find someone, there are video tutorials online. This is, unfortunately, one of those things a book can't entirely convey. Seeing a professional in action is the best way to learn and save you and your goat a lot of trouble.

Milking

The end result of all this effort is to have a doe ready for milking. If you mimic the way cows are milked in cartoons, you are going to end up with a kicked bucket and a severely peeved goat. Any homesteader who buys kids must wait at least two years to get milk, but adult does may be ready to milk the day they are brought home.

Milking is something of an art. It can take hours or ten minutes, depending on the doe and the hands milking her. Start by leading the doe to the milking station and coaxing her into a stanchion with some grain.

A stanchion is a wooden restraint that gently holds a goat's head in place. It is not cruel and makes the milking process easier for doe and milker alike. You can buy them, but they are not something sold at the local strip mall, and it is sometimes easier to just make one. A basic stanchion is stable and has a rotating or sliding plank that can be locked into place behind the jaw and ears.

When the goat is secured, sit down on a stool and place a sterilized bucket underneath her. The best buckets are seamless, stainless steel. Massage her teats with a soft towel dipped in bleach or iodine, or dip

186

them in a solution of either. If your doe has hairy teats, a quick shave makes everything more sanitary.

Massaging the teats stimulates milk flow, and after a few minutes they should begin to fill with milk. Cut off that flow by wrapping your thumb and forefinger at the base of the teat and squeezing. Twisting very gently helps seal it off. Still keeping firm pressure at the base, begin squeezing down the teat, first with the middle finger, then the ring finger, and finally the pinky. Never pull: it hurts the doe and damages her udder.

If done right, the milk should flow out of the teat. Squirt the first stream from each teat away from the bucket for hygiene. Then release your hold on the teat, allowing it to refill, and repeat, this time into the bucket.

Milk twice a day, and be aware of the consequences for missing a milking. Neglected udders become swollen and painful and are more prone to developing mastitis later in life. Having a doe in milk means no vacations, no sleeping in, and no late nights out without the guarantee that someone will be there to take care of her.

Goats are an excellent starting point for other livestock because of their size and usefulness. Meat goats, cows, pigs, and more are explored in year four, and many of the principles learned with goats will show up again later.

POULTRY II

Having a few different kinds of poultry on the property is a good thing. Chicken, though a delicious meal, eventually becomes bland and unappetizing when it's the only meat on the menu. Simple living should expand your horizons, not limit them.

This chapter covers raising chickens for the table but also the other domesticated fowl that add some flavor and diversity to the barnyard. They range in size from a few ounces to more than 40 pounds.

Much of what you know about caring for chickens is applicable to other poultry, but key differences are noted as part of their care instructions.

Broilers

The best chickens for meat are Cornish Cross broilers. These hybrids have been developed for decades to grow at a phenomenal pace, more than three times as fast as the average dual-purpose bird. They convert feed to pounds more efficiently and develop the plentiful breast meat Americans have come to expect from their chicken.

By comparison, dual-purpose breeds like the Sussex or the Rhode Island Red are downright scrawny. A Cornish Cross at eight weeks is larger and tenderer than a dual-purpose bird at 20. In their favor, the dual-purpose chickens are healthier and breed true generation after generation.

Try raising a batch of each to decide what is right for you. Chickens raised on pasturage taste far better than anything at the grocery store.

Caponizing

Before the Cornish Cross entered the scene in the '50s and '60s, capons were the meat birds of choice. They are cockerels castrated at a young age. As a result, they grow larger while remaining tender and docile, like a plump hen. There are even stories of capons hatching and mothering chicks.

The only trouble with capons is caponizing: the process of removing the testicles. An incision is made between the ribs, which are then spread with a specialized instrument. The testicles are carefully removed and the bird is set free to recover, usually without stitches. It's a quick job for anyone who's experienced, but fatalities are common and a novice can cause inexcusable agony to the cockerel before death.

Pick up a dedicated kit, practice on dead birds, and have an expert demonstrate before attempting this invasive surgery. There's no point caponizing a Cornish Cross, but any dual-purpose bird will benefit. Jersey Giants in particular were famed as capons.

Broiler Housing

Keep young broilers in a brooder for at least their first two weeks of life. They can go outside once daytime temperatures are in the high 70s, but a heat lamp must be used for cooler nights. Raising them in summer saves bedding costs, so long as they also have access to fresh water at all times to avoid overheating as they grow. This is especially true for the Cornish Cross.

A chicken tractor is an economical way to save on bedding, keep broilers safe, and give them fresh grass to scratch through and eat. Tractors give chicks a reason to move around, which reduces the risk of heart attacks and muscular atrophy.

A tractor's main design traits are portability and sturdiness. It is a wooden or PVC structure lined with chicken wire or hardware cloth. One section is covered to provide shade and shelter from the elements. An extension cord can be used to power a heat lamp, but that lamp needs to be kept out of the rain.

Broiler tractors are used because of the sheer amount that the Cornish Cross eat and, by extension, excrete. Feed and bedding costs can quickly turn a batch of chickens into a money pit. By moving them around and giving them pasture to scratch, both expenses are greatly reduced.

Feeding Broilers

Dual-purpose cockerels are often raised on standard layer feed as extras with the pullets. Broilers, having been purchased specially for the table, are given a high-protein diet. This can be purchased bagged at many farm supply stores or at a feed mill.

Broiler starter is fed for the first six weeks of life, at about 23 percent protein. They are then switched over to broiler finisher at 19 percent. This finisher is fed until they reach the desired slaughter weight.

Feeding broilers 24/7 yields larger birds, but it's also risky. They are the ultimate gluttons and are happy to fall asleep with their heads in the feeder. Uninhibited access to feed may cause weight gain faster than their bodies can keep up. Offer feed for 12 hours and then withhold it for another 12 to manage growth.

Slaughtering a Chicken

Cornish Cross are slaughtered between six and 10 weeks of age. Most dual-purpose breeds are slaughtered at 16 to 20. In between are what are called "slow broilers," which are processed at around 12.

When a bird is ready for the table, it must be killed, scalded, eviscerated, and cleaned. If you have raised rabbits and already slaughtered a litter, this should be familiar. Otherwise, it is difficult for many people, especially the first time. Only process one chicken to begin with, giving yourself time to figure it out without any pressure.

There are many ways to kill a chicken, but the quickest and most humane methods both involve severing the major arteries in the neck.

The first is old-fashioned but practical. The chicken's neck is outstretched on a level, wooden platform, either by hand or between two nails. Then the head is separated from the body with a hatchet. The chicken is hung by the feet and allowed to bleed out.

The second, and my preferred method, is to suspend the chicken in a "killing cone" and then cut the throat with a sharp knife. Being upside down disorients and calms the cockerel, preventing a struggle, and it's harder to mess up a firm knife stroke than a hatchet swing. In addition, the carcass can be left in the cone to bleed out with no additional bother.

A large traffic cone is a cheap tool for this. Simply detach the base, cut the top down to fit a chicken, and nail it to a tree or post. Place a bucket underneath to catch the blood. The finished cone, complete with chicken, should look like the picture on the previous page.

Before processing, heat a large pot up to 150 degrees, plus or minus five. Too hot will begin to cook the bird, but too cool won't loosen the feathers.

Grab the chicken by the head and gently pull down. Slice across the throat right underneath the jaw line with a sharp knife. If done right, there should be an immediate spurt of blood and the chicken will lose consciousness as his brain is deprived of oxygen. Death follows within minutes. Let the chicken hang until the blood has stopped flowing. At that point, the chicken must be scalded or skinned. I choose to scald to save the delicious skin, but removing everything is quicker.

Scalding loosens the feathers and also dislodges any remaining blood. Dunk the chicken into the water you heated prior to slaughtering, making sure to submerge the entire bird. Pull on the feathers after a few moments. If they aren't easily removed, submerge it again. Once you can pull out the feathers by hand without tearing the skin, begin plucking.

This is the most time-consuming part of processing. If you plan to process hundreds of birds a year, consider building a home-made plucker. Otherwise, you'll be pulling thousands of feathers out by hand. There's no need to pluck the neck and head, unless you plan to use them in cooking.

Once the chicken is bald, wash it off in a sink or with a hose to remove any last bits of debris. Next, take off the feet with a sharp knife. This is easy to do if you work through the joint at the hock. The neck is a little bit trickier. Cut through underneath the head. There will be some tubes sticking out of the remaining neck, including one leading to the crop, where a chicken's food is stored right after eating. If the chicken has been allowed feed before slaughter, the crop will be apparent on the right side of the chest. If not, it is a cleaner removal but harder for beginners to track down.

Start by filleting the skin of the neck open to reveal the esophagus and trachea. The esophagus is smoother and softer. Follow the esophagus down into the body, where it connects with the crop. Carefully work it free by twisting and pulling. You may need to loosen it with a finger, but keep working at it and it will eventually come free.

Next, remove the neck by pulling back the skin at

its base to reveal where it meets the body. Slice at this area and then twist the neck to pull it loose. The chicken should now be looking a lot more like something from the grocery store. Take a minute to clean up any extra skin and wash it again.

Before removing the internal organs, cut the tail off. This is done to carve out a small scent gland located in the tail, which flavors the meat as it sits. Most people prefer to avoid this flavor. The gland is a bump at the base of the tail.

The organs are removed by cutting a hole around the vent. Pinch the skin at the vent and make a small opening with a sharp knife. Do not puncture deeply and be careful not to hit any organs. Then use your fingers to expand the opening until you can fit your hand inside the cavity.

Be aware that, as this happens, waste may escape the intestines. This is the primary reason why broilers are not fed prior to slaughter. It smells very badly, but as long as it does not get on the meat it will not impact flavor. Handle the intestines carefully and do not break them if at all possible.

With the chicken on its back, reach in and begin carefully pulling out the internal organs. There is one organ, besides the intestines, that you absolutely do not want to break, and that is the gall bladder. The gall bladder produces bile and is easy to spot thanks to its greenish tint. It is small and pointed. Always make sure that it has been removed in one piece. If it breaks, the bile spoils the meat.

Start examining the internal organs of the chicken as you process. It is a good lesson in anatomy and will make spotting discrepancies easier in the future. The last organ out is the intestine, still attached to the vent. To remove it, cut a hole around the vent and pull it away from the body. When the cavity is mostly clean, the lungs will probably still be in place. They are attached to the chicken's back and can be pried out with your fingers or a lung scraper. Once everything is gone, rinse out the interior and give the body itself a final wash.

Vacuum seal chickens, use shrinking bags, or keep them in large sandwich bags for storage. Don't plan to eat the chicken the night you kill it. Rigor mortis sets in soon after death and take a few days in the fridge to wear off.

This slaughtering process applies to most poultry and is also broadly applicable to larger mammals, which will be covered in greater detail later.

Burn the remains you do not use, feed them to hogs or other chickens, or place them at the very center of a secure compost heap.

Ducks

Ducks are overshadowed by chickens in popular consumption, despite being their equals in egg and meat production. Their need for fresh water is their greatest limiting factor, but large and flavorful eggs, combined with crisp, succulent meat, are more than enough reason for the minimal investment.

Popular Breeds

Like chickens, there are a wide variety of bantam and standard ducks. For the purposes of this book, however, only the standards will be considered. Every domesticated duck besides the Muscovy is descended from the common mallard, pictured above.

Khaki-Campbells and Indian Runners are preferred laying breeds. Indian Runners are tall, lithe ducks that need ample space to stretch their legs. They have somewhat nervous temperaments but produce very large eggs. Khaki-Campbells are more familiar-looking and docile. Both breeds produce 300 or more eggs a year, better than the best chickens.

The most popular meat breed is the Pekin. They are nervous birds but also better at sustaining their population than the Cornish Cross. The other common meat duck is the Muscovy. Muscovies are substantially larger than Mallard-based ducks, reaching as much as 15 pounds. They roost like chickens, brood their eggs, and are quite hardy, making them a good fit for homesteads.

Duck Housing

Ducks need access to water to breed, clean themselves, and generally be happy as instinctive waterfowl. Besides some sort of pond, you must also give them basic shelter as protection against predators and the elements.

Some owners let a few ducks sleep in the chicken coop. A three-sided hutch with at least two square feet per duck is fine so long as it is secure from predators and the flock is able to come and go at will. Just like chicken coops, ventilation is of primary importance in duck housing. As waterfowl, ducks are perfectly capable of withstanding some wind and rain, but humidity is a killer.

A duck pond doesn't have to be large for a small

flock, so long as the ducks have room to paddle around, breed, and moisten their feathers. A hard plastic kiddie pool works well and is easy to clean, but obviously a full-sized pond is preferable. Plan for 25 ducks per acre of water to maintain plant and insect populations. The minimum depth for ducks is 8".

Ducklings are raised in a brooder, much like chicks, only they have a reputation for making messes. Water fountains are seen as a great opportunity to splash around, meaning their bedding gets wet quickly. For that reason, ducklings tend to get moved outside faster than chicks.

Feeding Ducks

Finding packaged duck feed is sometimes a difficult proposition. Explore local feed stores, but if none carry it on the shelf, you should be able to find at least one that can order it for you. A feed mill may also have it.

As with chickens, ducks are fed starter, grower, and finisher formulas crafted for both meat and laying breeds. Free ranging ducks pick up bugs and plants, especially those in ponds, and can cover a substantial portion of their own diet.

Raising Ducks

Worm ducks once a year and watch them for signs of other illnesses. Wild ducks stopping by the pond are common carriers of disease.

Ducks are more haphazard about laying than chickens. You might have to engage in some foraging every day to find them. When raised for meat, ducks are slaughtered and processed just like chickens, though their feathers are harder to pluck. Adding a squirt of dish detergent to the scalding pot helps loosen them.

Geese

Geese are an uncommon sight on farms simply because there are other poultry that are easier to raise. They are, however, a useful bird to have, especially in orchards, where they act as mowers and clean up fallen fruits. Goose was once the traditional Christmas meal and, though now a rarity, is a delicious meat.

Geese can be aggressive animals and should not be allowed around small children or other poultry.

Goose Breeds

Two of the most common breeds are the Embden and the Toulouse. Both are large, heavyset geese that mature to about 20 pounds.

Goose Housing

Like ducks, geese need water to splash about, breed, and clean themselves in. Their size means that they require deeper water than ducks. A small above-ground pool or pond should be sufficient, so long as it's at least 12" deep.

Again like ducks, geese need at least a rudimentary shelter to stay out of the elements at night, though they are very hardy. Unlike ducks, they cannot be housed in a chicken coop because of their greater size and strength.

Feeding Geese

Geese are herbivores that love fresh green grass. If kept pastured, they provide most of their own sustenance. Supplement their scavenging with a waterfowl or game bird feed.

Raising Geese

Geese are very much an optional livestock. Some are sweet and docile, but they can become aggressive as they age. If you have the resources for them, they are excellent table birds and very popular around the holidays. If not, you may have better luck with other poultry.

Guineafowl

Guineas are the oddities of the poultry world. They are roughly the size of a chicken but more closely related to pheasants and turkeys. They originated in Africa and are an independent bird best known for their loud cries when confronted with the unknown. Guineas are raised as watchdogs, natural insect control, and for their meat.

Guinea Housing

It is nearly impossible to keep guineas contained, as they are decent flyers and have an inclination to roam. They can be taught to return to a coop at night and roost with chickens, but they often revert to sleeping in trees. This leaves them vulnerable to owls and other night predators and should be discouraged.

During the day, most flock owners let their guineas roam the property. They are especially useful for controlling the population of ticks and other invasive bugs. You will lose a few to predators if the farm isn't secure, and anyone with close neighbors should reconsider owning guineas. There is nothing quite like waking up to twenty shrieking birds in the driveway.

Feeding Guineas

Guineas given free range find much of their own food. There are few, if any, commercially available guinea feeds, so you will have to wing it and trust that they will forage any lacking nutrients. Feed keets (juveniles) game bird starter with protein levels at about 25 percent. Reduce their feed's protein levels to 20 percent at six weeks and 16 percent at 15.

Raising Guineas

Guineas are fairly easy to look after once they've been trained to roost in a coop. They bully chickens if kept in a run with them and even occasionally interbreed.

Guinea hens lay their eggs in private, hidden nests and eventually brood once the clutch is large enough. Assuming they are not found by a predator, the eggs hatch in about 25 days. Guinea hens are dubious mothers at times, so it may be smarter to collect the keets and put them in a brooder.

Sexing guineas is not as simple as with other poultry. The males and females look almost the same, except for the males' enlarged wattles and helmet. Hens also make a distinctive "Buck-wheat" sound.

Guineas are a love-them-or-hate-them sort of poultry. If you can, find someone with a flock to ensure that you can handle their noisy squawks before setting them loose on the property.

Quail

Quail are the rabbits of poultry. They are tiny, reproduce quickly, and shouldn't be discounted for their diminutive size. These little birds are a fast and easy meat source that do not require half an acre to raise.

Quail Breeds

Check local regulations before ordering quail. Some states and counties restrict their ownership.

The bobwhite is the most familiar type of quail. They are wild and grow slowly, but common consensus is that their all-white meat tastes better than any other quail. They reach slaughter age at about 20 weeks and lay approximately 100 eggs a year. Bobwhites are more aggressive and need larger housing to prevent cannibalism.

The other quail breed of note is the coturnix. Coturnix quail lay approximately 300 eggs per year and are ready to slaughter in eight weeks. They are much more docile than bobwhites and do not have the picking problems seen in their cousins. Whether their speedy production and headache-free handling is worth slightly inferior meat is up to you.

Most feed stores do not offer quail, but hatcheries

and breeders sell both eggs and live chicks.

Quail Housing

Because of their size, quail cannot be kept in the same conditions as other poultry. Most are raised in cages or hutches, about three feet high and with one or two square feet per bird. Larger operations use sheds with fine mesh covering all ventilation openings. Dirt or wood shavings protect a quail's feet and give it something to scratch around in.

Quail chicks should be raised in a brooder with ½ square feet per chick.

Feeding Quail

Quail do best on a game bird feed. Give chicks a starter formula until they are six weeks old. Quail raised for meat should then be switched over to a grower formula, and those kept for breeding to a laying formula. Like chickens, any quail given treats need grit first to aid digestion.

Raising Quail

A single quail is about 150 calories of low-fat, protein-dense meat. Their prolific laying and quick development means that it is easy to keep up a constant rotation of birds to stock the freezer.

Keep breeder quail at a ratio of at least three females per male and collect eggs daily. A good incubator holds at least 50 quail eggs at a time, but some can hatch hundreds. Watch for signs of disease, which can wipe out an entire pen in a few days. Afflicted birds must be quarantined immediately.

Turkeys

Most families only eat turkey on the holidays and in sandwiches, but this ultimate meat bird is delectable year-round. The turkeys raised by the commercial industry are big, bland and a bit stupid, but even they taste far better when raised in a farm setting and allowed to forage for themselves.

Turkey Breeds

The most common turkeys today are the giant broad-breasted whites, which can grow to weigh 40 pounds or more. They are akin to broiler chickens in growth rate and feed efficiency, but they share similar health problems as well. They are ready to slaughter at around 20 weeks.

Heritage breeds are more sustainable but less

efficient. They typically take closer to 25 or 30 weeks to reach butchering age and dress out smaller. They are, however, more cunning and likely to rear replacement poults (juveniles). The Bronze, Bourbon Red, and Narragansett are the most popular alternatives to the broad-breasted white.

Turkey Housing

There is some debate on housing turkeys with other poultry. Chickens sometimes carry a disease known as Blackhead, which is relatively harmless for them but potentially deadly in turkeys. Some farmers raise the two side by side without issue, but it's safer to give turkeys their own quarters.

Turkeys are less domesticated than chickens. They roost in trees if allowed and spend their days scavenging through the undergrowth much like their wild ancestors. The heritage breeds can be nearly self-sufficient if given enough space. A large pasture with at least 500 square feet per bird, 200 if they are rotated, is the best way to support a flock, but may not be feasible for your small farm.

Instead, a few turkeys can also be kept in a run or in "turkey tractors." Turkeys kept with chickens will roost in the coop or even on its roof. They are hardy, if lacking in common sense, and need little more than a place to sleep, eat, and drink in safety.

Turkey poults, like all poultry, are kept in a brooder if not raised by their mother.

Feeding Turkeys

Turkeys are raised on game bird or specialized turkey feed. As might be expected from their size, they can eat you off the farm in no time, which is why so many turkey owners choose to raise them on pasture. Even the best free-ranging flock, however, needs daily access to feed.

Turkey poults should be fed starter crumbles until they are six to eight weeks old. Then a grower formula is used from 12 to 15 weeks, and a finisher is fed until slaughter.

Raising Turkeys

Turkeys are essentially the polar opposites of quail: big and in need of plenty of space. Many homestead turkeys end up free ranging over the property, but they are vulnerable to predation. Bigger turkeys take care of themselves to an extent, but foxes, coyotes, and dogs overpower them. Pasturing and tractoring are better solutions.

Turkeys are ready to slaughter when they have a healthy layer of fat under their skin. This fat is what keeps them moist in the oven. Butcher turkeys with the same killing cone method as chickens, though you will need the largest cone size possible for the big toms. The processing methods between chickens and turkeys are identical.

CANNING AND FOOD STORAGE

The problem with gardens is that they are seasonal and sometimes unpredictable. Gardeners are overrun with vegetables and fruits in the summer and then left wanting in the winter. Back when families relied on their farms and had few safety nets, they faced starvation without preserves. Learning how to can and store food safely will keep you fed throughout the lean, cold months and power outages.

Before the technological revolution pushed families off the land and into cities and suburbs, the fall harvest was second only to spring planting as the most important time of the year. The majority of the foods gathered were put away to feed the homestead. They carried everyone through until the spring crops began producing enough to live off of.

In all likelihood, you will underestimate how much you need to store this first year. That's a natural part of the learning process. Document how much you store, and when you run out of it, for future reference.

Canning

Canning is the process of eliminating harmful organisms within a jar of food. Some die quick, but others thrive in heat and slip through if you are not careful. When this happens, the results can be terrible, and even deadly, so exercise caution at all times.

Canning is performed by heating and pressurizing the contents of a jar thoroughly. How long that takes depends on the food's density and pH. A jar full of vinegar, for example, takes almost no time at all.

For safety's sake, buy yourself a pressure canner. These are the only devices that can heat foods with a high pH to the necessary temperatures. Water-bath canning is faster and safe for use in acidic foods like fruits and pickles, but to can anything more alkaline than tomatoes you must use a pressure canner.

Necessary Items

- Pressure canner
- Canning pot
- Canning rack
- Canning jar lifter
- Pint or quart glass jars (Mason or similar)
- Lids and rings for the jars

Before Canning

Before you begin, prepare the food as instructed in whatever recipe you are following. Some call for cooking the food first (hot packing), but usually you will just be dicing it up into smaller pieces or canning whole (raw packing). There should be no visible bruises, mold, or other signs of decay on the food in question. Sometimes problem spots can be scooped out, but never can subpar produce.

Clean your jars prior to use and inspect them for nicks and cracks. The slightest opening allows contamination. Also check the rings and lids. Lids MUST be new, and the rings must be straight and seal tightly. Jars cannot be larger than one quart for safe canning. Wash them with soap and hot water, and then run them through the dishwasher or scalding water. To sterilize them, boil in water for at least 10 minutes. Allow them to dry.

Never cause a sudden temperature shift in glass jars. Before placing them in the canner, heat them up in a hot water bath. Similarly, do not place cold foods in a hot jar. Glass is prone to shattering upon expansion or contraction and can cause serious injury if not handled carefully.

If your produce needs a liquid, prepare it according to your recipe. This is also the time to begin boiling a water-bath kettle. Place the food and its liquid in the jar, leaving headspace as specified in the recipe. Use a wooden ladle to remove any and all air bubbles.

Heat up the lids, but do not boil them. Wipe off the rim of the jar with a clean, soapy towel, then place the hot lids on the rim and tighten by hand with the ring. At this point, it's time to place them in either the water-bath or pressure canner.

Water-Bath Canning

Water-bath canning is the most basic type and can be done with minimal equipment. Once the water in the canning kettle is boiling, place the jars on the canning rack and gently lower it into the canner. The water will stop boiling and should be at least 1" above the lids. When the water begins boiling again, start timing. Always follow the recipe when in doubt, but the table at the end of this section also lists general cooking times.

Pressure Canning

Pressure canning also uses boiling water, but the jars are not immersed in it. Instead, steam builds up pressure inside the sealed canner. Since steam can reach higher temperatures than water, the pressure canner easily manages 240 degrees. Because pressure canners are your only line of defense against botulism, have yours tested every year for accuracy. As always, your local extension office can help you.

Pressure canners are not a fail-safe piece of equipment, so always re-read the manual and stay on your toes. Pour in as much water as the instructions dictate. There should be a basket to place the jars in to keep them off of direct heat.

Close the canner's lid and begin applying heat. Eventually steam will begin to pour from the vent. Once a steady stream has been ongoing for 10 minutes, close the vent and wait for the pressure to rise to the right level based on your recipe. You will probably need to fiddle with your heat source to keep it in the sweet spot. Start timing when it reaches the correct pressure, and never let it fall below that once you begin canning.

After the allotted time, take the canner off the

heat and let it cool with the jars for approximately an hour. Never remove the lid while the pressure is above zero or steam is still emitting from the canner. Even after an hour, be extremely careful when opening up a pressure canner. First, open the valve and let more hot air escape. Then slowly remove the lid. Do not stand or place any body part directly over the canner, as the steam may burn you. Let the canner stand for another 15 minutes before removing the jars.

Cooling

Pull out each jar with the jar lifter and allow them to cool in a safe place. Do not touch them during this process, as they are still sealing. You should hear them pop as the seal is finalized. This is the result of the changing temperatures forming a vacuum and sucking the lid down against the rim.

Place hot jars on a soft, warm surface like a towel while they cool. Do not touch them for 24 hours. To check the seal, push against the lid. If it dents and pops back up, it has failed. You can try again with a new lid or toss it.

When it comes time to move them to storage, there's no need to keep the rings on. The lids' seals should be more than enough. Keep jars in a cool, dry, and dark area. Attics and cellars work well.

Safety

Please remember that this is only a basic guide to canning. Read and follow all instructions on your canner and in your recipes. When in doubt, don't leave it up to chance. Canning is an excellent way to store foods, but it is also the most dangerous and people do die from poor practices.

When opening up a canned item, check that the seal is in place. You should hear the rush of air entering a vacuum. Eyeball the food and give it a good sniff. If it doesn't seem right, throw it away. Follow your intuition and all safety instructions, and with any luck you will never have to deal with a virulent or painful infection or accident.

The chart on the next page uses information from the USDA's "Complete Guide to Home Canning.[17]" It's a free download that I recommend to anyone as a comprehensive source on the subject. All numbers are for raw goods at altitudes below 1000 feet, unless otherwise labeled.

Canning Times

Food	Water-Bath or Pressure	Time – Pint (Minutes)	Time – Quart (Minutes)
Apples	Water-Bath	20	20
Asparagus	Pressure	30	40
Beans (Hot)	Pressure	75	90
Beets (Hot)	Pressure	30	35
Berries	Water-Bath	15	20
Carrots	Pressure	25	30
Cherries	Water-Bath	20	25
Corn	Pressure	55	85
Peaches	Water-Bath	25	30
Pears (Hot)	Water-Bath	20	25
Peas	Pressure	40	40
Peppers (Hot)	Pressure	35	-
Plums	Water-Bath	20	25
Potatoes (Hot)	Pressure	35	40
Rhubarb (Hot)	Water-Bath	15	15
Spinach (Hot)	Pressure	70	90
Squash (Hot)	Pressure	55	90
Tomatoes	Pressure	25	25

Drying

Drying was the preservation method of choice before the invention of canning and is still useful in many situations. It works by desiccating a fruit, vegetable or piece of meat and halting the growth of bacteria by depriving them of water.

The oldest form of drying is to place something out in the sun. This can lead to airborne pollutants and insects entering your food supply, so I recommend using a dehydrator whenever possible.

Many foods lend themselves well to drying. Beans, fruits like apples and apricots, herbs, peas, and beef are some of the most popular, but try everything once.

Preparing Foods

Any large items must be sliced to fit into the average dehydrator. Most foods are intuitive: make apricot donuts, beef strips, and zucchini chips.

Clean everything thoroughly before it goes in. Fruits can be dehydrated as soon as they are sliced, but some people like to dip them in salt water or ascorbic acid beforehand. You can also create fruit leathers by blending fruits into a liquid and pouring the result onto a non-stick surface in the dehydrator.

Vegetables are blanched prior to dehydrating, either by steam or boiling. The time needed varies by vegetable, but they should be tender and nicely cooked. After that, the vegetables are plunged into an ice-water bath and dried thoroughly with paper towels.

Meat takes a bit more work. First, it must be heated to at least 165 degrees prior to dehydrating. The meat should be lean and cut into thin slices. Slice against the grain to make it tenderer. Seasoning or marinating beforehand improves both flavor and texture. Curing is an ancient tradition where meat is either salted or smoked to preserve it. Some dry sausages can store at room temperature for months or even years.

Store dried foods loosely packed in a jar or bag. Keep them away from moisture. You can either eat dried foods as a snack or rehydrate them to use in cooking.

Freezing

Freezing is quick and easy, but unreliable. Don't put all your eggs in one basket, as they say, but there's no denying the usefulness of a good chest freezer. A freezer should keep its contents at slightly less than zero degrees Fahrenheit. Staying well below the freezing point allows them to keep longer.

Most raw fruits and blanched vegetables store for about a year in a freezer. Raw meat averages about six months. Store them in heavy-duty bags, jars, or plastic.

Defrost the freezer once a year by scraping off the frost layer with a plastic tool. If it refuses to come off, turn off the power and add hot water in bowls. Scrub the interior, dry it, and plug the freezer back in.

Foods coming out of the freezer should always be defrosted in a fridge and not in open air.

Storing in a Root Cellar

Not everything needs to be frozen, heated, or pressurized. Many vegetables last for months if kept in a cool, dark, and dry area. Old houses were built with root cellars for this purpose, and it's a worthwhile project to dig one. Basements make for good storage, but they are probably too warm to function as a root cellar without insulation.

A basic root cellar is dug into the side of a north-facing slope. Once the hole is large enough, supporting timbers are installed and the roof is covered with plastic sheeting and dirt. A door and some form of ventilation completes the structure. The earth keeps the temperatures cool in both summer and winter.

Line the cellar with shelves and bins. Legumes, cabbages, onions, peppers, squashes, potatoes, apples, pears, turnips, radishes, and parsnips all store for months if kept away from moisture.

Watch the cellar for pests, which love nothing more than a safe larder filled with food. Rodents and insects are a sign of entry points that need to be filled in and should be eliminated as quickly as possible to protect your stores.

HUNTING AND FISHING

Every year, hunters across the nation spend hours in the wilderness and, hopefully, return home with some of the finest and cheapest meat available anywhere.

There are plenty of ethical considerations regarding hunting and fishing, but from personal experience those who will raise a domestic animal to eat are not opposed to slaughtering a wild one. If you are the exception, you are not going to starve if you forego either sport.

Even if you don't go hunting or fishing every year, it's smart to know the basics. Anyone with more than an acre likely sees animal traffic regularly, and this is one survival skill that could always prove handy.

Hunting

Whether it be from deer, boar, waterfowl, or even larger game, the meat gained from hunting can feed a family for weeks or months at little cost. Anyone can shoot an animal. The real difficulty lies in the preparation beforehand. An experienced hunter is well-versed in local laws, gun safety, luring in animals, making a clean kill, and then processing the carcass.

Before doing anything else, learn what can be done in your area. Find out education requirements and fees for a license. Look up what you can kill, when you can kill it, and how many you can kill. It's only when you are armed with that knowledge that you can continue making plans.

Safety

Guns are a superb tool when used properly, but all too often they are not. Hunting programs in the United States now emphasize safety for the benefit of all hunters and citizens.

Follow basic rules while out hunting: Keep the safety on and never fire unless you have a clear line of sight to your target. Wear safety equipment and don't shoot at the sound of an animal. Don't take wild shots: You will miss and may endanger others. Finally, follow up on every shot, even if you think you missed.

There is more to safety while hunting than minding your gun, of course. If you use a tree stand, stay strapped in at all times and use a pulley system to retrieve your weapons and gear. Always use caution when approaching a downed animal. Even if it's not moving, treat it as though it is still alive and dangerous until you have confirmed otherwise. Pay attention for other hunters in your area.

Finally, let people know where you will be and how long you intend to be gone, especially if you are heading into back country. Stick to land that you know and have permission to use.

Rifle Hunting

Rifles are the most versatile weapons for taking game. They offer long-distance precision and power, making them valuable for spooky animals such as deer. Most modern hunting rifles are scoped for accuracy.

Rifle hunting is usually a waiting game. The hunter disguises him- or herself as best as possible along a known game trail and then makes a shot once the prey walks past. Game may be lured in with calls or trained to frequent the area with regular baiting.

Shotgun Hunting

Shotguns are the traditional weapon of choice

when hunting fowl, both ground and water, and many other game. Hunters using shotguns find their quarry and then flush them out with either dogs or a partner. The shotgun offers a wide spread of projectiles, increasing the chances of hitting a rapidly moving target.

Bow Hunting

Bow hunting is seeing a resurgence in popularity as a more demanding way to take game. In most states, bow hunting also has its own season before the firearm hunters, giving archers an advantage.

Without the firepower of a gun, bow hunters need to be much closer to their prey. A common method is to use tree stands, which were later adopted as a popular strategy for rifle hunters as well. There is even the sport of bow fishing.

Primitive Hunting

Bows and arrows may seem like a journey into the third century, but primitive hunting extends into prehistory. It is most often practiced by experienced hunters looking for a challenge. There are many weapons to choose from, ranging from slings to spears, dating back to the earliest hunter-gatherer societies. This hunting is dangerous and exhilarating and not for the faint of heart.

Hunting with Dogs

Dogs are mankind's oldest domesticated companions, and they have been helping with the hunt for thousands of years. The best of them are smart, agile, and relentless.

Certain breeds have been selected for their ability to hunt. The sight hounds, such as Greyhounds, are lean and fast to capture rabbits and other small prey. Gun dogs like the Labrador Retriever or German Shorthaired Pointer find, flush, and retrieve fowl. Members of the hound group typically use their strong sense of smell to track prey and hold it at bay. Physically strong breeds like the American Pit Bull Terrier or American Bulldog are also used to pin down aggressive game like boars.

Working with a hunting dog develops a bond of

trust and understanding most dog owners will never experience. I recommend taking a training course with your dog even if you never plan to actually practice the skills.

Trapping

The last method widely used today is trapping. This includes the use of live traps and snares. They are less time-intensive than other types of hunting but need a specialized knowledge to be effective. It may be wise to keep live traps around your homestead to control the local predator population, but snares can also bring in a steady supply of rabbit and other meat if needed.

Fishing

Fishing is a favorite pastime that can prove to be quite rewarding with dedication. You may event want to create your own pond and stock it with fish for easier access. Most streams, rivers, lakes, and coastlines require a fishing license and observance of designated fishing seasons. As with hunting, human beings have found many ways to catch fish over the years.

Angling

By far the most popular method among small-scale fishers today, fishing with a rod and hook is the standard strategy for most species. Certain fish are best caught with different types of angling, such as fly or lure fishing. Find out which species are in your local waterways and buy your gear accordingly.

Netting

Netting is the act of capturing a fish from the bank or a boat with some sort of mesh. It's how the commercial fishing industry operates, though individuals use much smaller nets. This method requires patience, speed, and a keen eye, but it eliminates the need to coax fish into accepting bait.

Spear Fishing

The original form of fishing, spear fishing is as basic as it gets. A sharpened stick or blade is thrust into the water and pins a fish. This is, perhaps, also the most difficult way to catch a fish due to the shifting of water and wariness of the prey.

Some fishermen have taken spears into the 21st century with spearguns, which fire at blinding speeds and allow deep-water hunting through extended dives.

YEAR FOUR

GARDENING IV

By your fourth year of homesteading, you should be able to supply most, if not all, of your family's vegetables and have a good idea of how much space you need.

As a consequence, this year and the year after it are primarily meant to increase your skills and experience. There are a hundred ways to lose a harvest for the year, and the more you see the more you will be able to deal with efficiently. After all, there's only so much a book can teach you; the real wealth of knowledge must be gained by getting outside and sifting through some dirt.

Instead of buying seeds every spring and relying on access to a nursery, begin collecting seeds and expanding winter crops. Both are relatively easy, giving you time to practice putting everything else together and maintain a sizable garden.

New Vegetables

By now, the common vegetables have mostly been covered, but don't limit yourself. Head to a local farmer's market and start exploring the varieties and quirky plants that thrive in your area.

These are the last vegetables I'll be covering in this book. They add more vegetarian sources of protein to the garden and several store well, making them valuable when meat is scarce or simply not on the menu.

Beans

Beans are occasionally overlooked by gardeners, but they should not be. The majority of them are fantastic for you and can be dehydrated and stored almost indefinitely. They are a staple of the farm diet.

There are two types of beans: bush and pole. Pole beans climb up supports, whether it on a trellis or corn stalks. Vine beans are grown essentially like peas, and this section is more dedicated to the bush beans, including kidney, pinto, soy, and black beans.

Soak bean seeds prior to planting to improve germination. Sow them outdoors, 1" deep, and thin them to at least 18" spacing.

Allow beans to remain on their plants until they have thoroughly dried out. A ripe bean is hard and dry to the touch; they dehydrate naturally. At this point they can be picked, separated from their husks, and stored.

Square feet per plant: 2.25

Plants per person: 5

Brussels Sprouts

Brussels sprouts have a reputation as the most "vegetable-y" of vegetables: the boogeyman of children everywhere. These relatives of the cabbage are a cool-season crop. The sprouts accumulate all along the stem of the plant, like bulbous growths, and taste best after experiencing a light frost. They are a fall crop in the warmer parts of the state.

Plant Brussels sprouts in slightly alkaline soil in mid-summer. Thin seedlings out to 24" spacing. Cut off the sprouts once they have reached mature size.

Square feet per plant: 4

Plants per person: 5

Rhubarb

Rhubarb pie is a sublime dessert, and the plant itself is an industrious, cold-loving perennial. It prefers average temperatures of less than 75 degrees and needs a dormancy period to begin growing in again in spring. The edible parts are the tart stalks, and the plant will continue to send up new growth for 15 years or more.

Purchase rhubarb as crowns for easier cultivation. Plant in partial shade to protect them from intense heat, with at least 36" between each crown. Trim back and divide the crowns as they spread to keep the rhubarb manageable. Do not harvest in the first year and only sparingly in the second. Once the rhubarb is established, cut stalks soon after the leaf spreads with a sharp knife.

Square feet per plant: 9

Plants per person: 1

Sunflowers

Sunflowers are valuable for their Vitamin D content and oil, which is used as a substitute for commercial cooking oils. They are also a good source of feed for livestock.

Sunflowers are hardy, so long as they are given plenty of water and sunlight. They prefer a soil pH of about 7.0 and do best with heavy fertilizing. Size and spacing depends on the variety, but plan for about 24" between the plants.

Harvest seeds when the sunflower heads are dry and brown. The seeds need additional drying, either by dehydrator or by spending a week in the sun. Store them in-shell in bags and check them regularly for signs of mold.

Square feet per plant: 4

Plants per person: 2

Harvesting Seeds and Plant Propagation

Growing vegetables in a standard garden is touted by most, including by myself, as an efficient and environmentally friendly form of food production, but it's still wasteful. Why? Because, at the end of the season, nearly every gardener in America tosses or tills his or her plants and prepares to buy seed packets next spring.

Granted, the seeds for even a large garden are unlikely to exceed $200, but expenses are expenses and there's always the question: What will you do if you can no longer buy seeds? With that in mind, you should begin collecting and saving seeds after harvesting a plant.

The procedure for each plant varies. This section covers every vegetable recommended previously in this book. Most of the information is pulled from personal experience, Carla Emry's constantly useful "The Encyclopedia of Country Living, [7]" and a handy guide published by the Seed Ambassadors Project.[18]

Propagation

It may be strange to think about engaging in plant husbandry, but it is vital to ensure that your garden remains strong and fertile. Varieties of plants that are pollinated by air or insect cannot be placed within ¼ mile of each other due to the potential of hybridization. Offspring from such hybrids lack genetic integrity and may be infertile. If you have a close neighbor with a garden, it is impossible to guarantee that some seeds are pure.

Choose the plants that grow the best produce, not only in quantity but also in quality and precociousness. Like animals, the best specimens should be given preference in reproduction to ensure strong future generations.

Modern GMO or hybridized seeds are not suitable for home propagation. In fact, it may be illegal depending on which company makes them. Also remember that even "self-pollinating" plants almost always need a pollinator, be it the wind or insects, to carry genetic material.

Artichokes

Artichokes bear viable seeds, but they are usually propagated by dividing the roots of a mature plant. Suckers, the shoots that come up around the roots, are able to survive on their own once they are about a foot tall. During the dormant seasons of fall or winter, cut straight down between the sucker and the larger plant with a sharp knife and gently remove it with a spade. Continue cutting as needed to avoid damaging the roots and then plant the crown in its new location.

The flower of the artichoke, the edible bit, continues to grow and dehydrate as seeds develop. Cut it off once brown and let it dry further. It won't let go of its seeds willingly, so stomp or smash it to loosen them.

Asparagus

An asparagus bed lasts for years and years, but sometimes seeds are needed to expand, replace poor performers, or refresh old plantings. As the spears are allowed to grow out in summer, the females develop small red berries that look a bit like miniature tomatoes. If you don't have any berries by fall, you probably have a garden full of male plants.

Once ripe, pick the berries and gently remove the seeds. Wash off the remaining pulp and sun them for a few weeks before storing.

Storage time: four years

Beets

Beets are part of a wide family, so be aware of any relatives in the garden. The most likely is Swiss Chard, and the two plants can cross-pollinate. Use bags or a wind-proof barrier if growing them together.

Beets take two years to produce seeds. Cut down the leaves in late fall and mulch heavily to help them survive the winter. Plan to save about 30 beets for harvest. The plants send up a stalk that can be picked when fully dried.

Storage time: five years

Broccoli

The brassica family can claim many popular members of the garden, and that causes problems with cross-pollination. Broccoli breeds with Brussels sprouts, cauliflower, cabbage, kale, and kohlrabi, among others. This means that they are almost impossible to save as seeds without careful management.

Broccoli gives seeds in its second spring. The pods are harvested once they are dry.

Storage time: five years

Brussels Sprouts

Much like the other brassicas, Brussels sprouts might be more trouble than they are worth. They interbreed with many other plants in the garden and must be isolated to ensure purity. Save the best of the plants and remove them to a safe place in winter. Transplant in spring. Cut the ensuing stalk when the majority of the pods are brown and then dry them for storage.

Storage time: five years

Cabbages

The process of saving cabbage seeds and the difficulties therein are almost identical to that of Brussels sprouts.

Storage time: five years

Carrots

Northern gardeners have a hard time getting a decent carrot crop through the frosts. There is also the problem of Queen Anne's Lace, a common wild carrot that gladly cross-pollinates.

Cover carrots in the late fall and then dig the tops back flush with the ground in spring. Harvest seeds once the stems are no longer green and then dry them further in a safe place.

Storage time: three years

Celery

Celery must also be stored in a frost-protected area during the winter. Place the entire plant in a pot, mulch, and set it back outdoors as soon as the danger is past. It will develop seeds either in early spring or late fall. These seeds have a tendency to drop off, so collect them regularly right off the plant.

Cut off the remaining flower heads and dry indoors to collect the rest.

Storage time: five years

Corn

Plant corn in blocks for more efficient pollination. Choose plants with the biggest and best ears for reproduction. Leave them until the corn inside is hard and dry but before the frosts hit.

Once they are ready, pick the ears and peel back the husk before suspending from a roof or shelf and allowing them to dry further. The seeds must have lost all traces of moisture before being removed from the cob.

Storage time: three years

Eggplant

Eggplants are as easy to breed as they are to grow. Keep the biggest and the fastest-maturing eggplants on the vine until they lose their sheen and become a brownish color. Then scoop out the seeds and pick them from the pulp. Adding water may help separate them. Dry before storage.

Storage time: five years

Garlic

The easiest way to propagate garlic is to save the cloves, which each grow into a new garlic plant. Dry the bulbs outdoors at less than 100 degrees Fahrenheit. The fat outer bulbs tend to be more virile than the thin ones at the center. Place them in a refrigerator, at temperatures higher than 32 degrees, for two months if planting in spring, otherwise sow in late fall as usual.

Garlic also puts out seeds, though like onions it can be a challenge to grow them. Much like their onion relatives, garlic plants send up a stalk that flowers and develops seeds in the fall.

Storage time: one to four years

Herbs

Most herbs develop a seed stalk or pods that are picked once brown and dry. Let them sun for a day or two and then store like other seeds.

Storage time: five years

Lettuce

Once the lettuces are nearing the end of their growing season, cease cutting leaves and let them send up stalks. They flower and, once pollinated, close again. Soon after, the buds produce fluffy fibers and open. Remove the buds and extract the seeds from their fibers.

Storage time: three years

Onions

Onions produce a single stalk bearing seeds after spending a winter in the ground. The seeds tend to blow away when ready, so either bag the flower after pollination or collect it early and dry indoors. These seeds must be stored in a cool, dry environment or they will expire quickly.

It's also possible to propagate onions by collecting the bulbs when they are the size of a large marble. Cut off the stalk and let the bulbs dry out in a sunny spot. Store them in a dark, cool, and dry place and then plant them in the spring. A cycle of collecting seeds, growing bulbs and then planting the next year reduces the difficulties of growing from seed alone.

Storage time: one year

Parsnips

Parsnips are resistant to cold, which makes overwintering them an easier proposition than other roots. Cut down the leaves and mulch them, much like beets and carrots, and they will bear seeds the next growing season.

Save plenty of these seeds to account for their finicky germination record.

Storage time: one year

Peppers

Peppers are a fruit, meaning their seeds are stored inside the edible portions. Hot and sweet varieties cross-pollinate, making it difficult for pepper-lovers to collect their seeds. They are self-pollinating and may be alright with 30 feet between varieties, but there's no guarantee that a curious bee won't start mingling pollens.

Pick the largest peppers and remove the seeds by cutting the fruits open at the bottom and scooping them out. Dry and store.

Storage time: five years

Pole Beans

Pole beans usually take care of themselves. Let the desired pods dry on the vine and then keep them as dry as possible throughout the winter.

Storage time: four years

Potatoes

Potatoes can be propagated in two ways. The preferred method is to simply save the biggest and best potatoes to be cut and sown in the spring. These are direct clones of the plants they came from and promise similar performance from generation to generation.

Potatoes also flower and produce seeds in small fruits, but they are more difficult to grow and offer little advantage to the average gardener.

Storage time: one year

Radishes

Radishes are so quick to develop that they bear seeds in just a few months. Let your "savers" remain in the ground until they send up stalks and seed pods. Once those pods are dry, they can be split open and the seeds removed. Fertile radish seeds are large and round.

Storage time: four years

Rhubarb

Rhubarb, like asparagus, is a perennial. It is propagated after it is at least five years of age by dividing the roots. This is easiest in early spring or late fall, when the growth is minimal. Dig up the root crown and divide it so that each new section has several buds and a good amount of root. Replant quickly to shock the plant as little as possible. Starting from seed is possible but not advised.

Storage time: hours

Rutabaga

Rutabaga, being a cross of turnip and cabbage, can obviously cross with both and put up seeds. It is a cold-loving plant and should overwinter with some mulch and shelter. Harvest seeds the following year.

Storage time: five years

Snap Peas

To save snap peas, pick the pods once they are large enough. Dry them out indoors or in sunlight before storing them shelled in a safe place. Peas are one of the best storing seeds thanks to their longevity.

Storage time: seven years

Spinach

Spinach likes cool weather. Once temperatures rise, it will naturally go to seed. There are male and female plants- you want the stalks with the largest seeds. Once the spinach plant is dry and yellow, uproot the stalk and strip the seeds.

Storage time: five years

Squash

Wait for squash to fully ripen before removing from the vine and then slice open and separate the seeds from the pulp. Dry in the sun before storage.

Storage time: five years

Swiss Chard

Swiss chard, as a type of beet, cross-pollinates with them if given the chance. They must be overwintered to produce seeds the next year. Use heavy mulch and hoophouses in colder climates. The chard sends up stalks and can be pulled up whole once the seeds are dry.

Storage time: five years

Tomatoes

Tomatoes rarely cross-pollinate each other, with the exception of potato-leaved varieties like the Brandywine. To clarify, growing standard or cherry tomatoes and Brandywines at a moderate distance should produce pure seeds most of the time.

Harvest seeds from ripe fruits. Place them in a container surrounded by the fruit's flesh with a bit of water, and let it sit for several days. Remove them before they begin to sprout, once the seeds begin to sink, then dry and store them.

Storage time: four years

Turnips

Turnips are another tricky plant when it comes to saving seed. Besides cross-pollinating with other plants, they are also sensitive to cold, meaning anyone with harsh winters must use mulch and a hoophouse or dig up the roots to store in a safe place. If you bring them indoors, store them in sand at around 37 degrees. They need a cold period for at least one month to flower.

Turnips send up tall stalks the following year and need two-foot spacing when propagating. Do not pull up the plant until the pods are dried.

Storage time: five years

Watermelons

Watermelons are an easy fruit to save. While eating a ripe melon, simply pull out the seeds and set them aside. Then wash them in water with a small squirt of dishwasher soap. The bad seeds float and should be discarded. Once they are clean, set them out in a sunny area to dry for approximately three weeks, stirring them occasionally.

Storage time: three years

Growing Year-Round

Having fresh vegetables in winter and early spring is a blessed relief after weeks and weeks of canned goods, especially when you start running low. All but the coldest climates can sustain a winter garden with the right help.

How long you can extend your growing season depends on your climate, garden setup, and the hardiness of your varieties. Hoop- and greenhouses are your first line of defense against the frost. They hold in heat and protect plants from snowfall or, worse, freezing rains. Mulch insulates the earth, shielding roots. Combined, they can bring plants through even freezing temperatures with little to no damage. Obviously, this is just as useful in early spring as it is in winter.

Cold hardy vegetables include: asparagus, beets, broccoli, cabbages, carrots, kale, kohlrabi, lettuce, onions, parsnips, peas, potatoes, radishes, spinach, and turnips.

ALTERNATIVE ENERGY II

Speaking of winters, living in the cold northern states is a major expense for homeowners, and even gentler climates have brisk nights to weather. Warming a home becomes a pricey proposition when chill air lurks just outside the windows.

With a bit of work and a willingness to make a few sacrifices, you don't need to spend hundreds or even thousands of dollars every winter to keep your toes attached to your feet. Our ancestors didn't have the luxury of an electric furnace to see them through the frosty months, and most of them still survived. Having the backup system of modern amenities does, however, ensure that you will in fact survive.

This section goes over how to heat your home through sustainable methods. Rather than relying on fossil fuels, you will be exploring renewable resources and energies, as well as how to winter-proof a home.

Reducing Heating Bills

Like many other aspects of self-sufficiency, the first thing to do when making the switch to alternative heating is to lower your consumption. This lessens the work and fuel required to keep your family comfortable. Even if you don't make a drastic switch quite yet, these steps should prove useful to lower your bills.

Insulating the House

Many houses today are built brittle, with the understanding that they can be piped full of heat to make up for their lack of insulation. These "cardboard" buildings are the most pressing, but even sturdy older homes benefit from a thermal-efficiency renovation.

Cold seeps through the thickest walls, but it is the cracks and thin points that are weakest. Windows are a major enemy in winter and leak huge amounts of energy if unprotected. Use duct tape or a more attractive professional seal to close gaps around their edges, and consider replacing them with multi-pane glass specifically designed to offer better insulation. Thick blinds or drapes also help keep heat in.

Repair any holes leading into the house, including ones in the attic. They are a direct route indoors for both vermin and cold air. Add more insulation to the attic, walls, and anywhere else applicable as needed.

Closing Off Rooms

Once, families closed off entire sections of their houses in winter. They did so to reduce their heating burden and sometimes slept together in the same bed for warmth. You don't need to do anything quite so cozy, of course, but the principle is still a sound one.

Determine which, if any, rooms you can do without for the season. Guest bedrooms are a common waste of heat. Seal off any vents and ducts leading into the room, as well as the windows. Then close the door and seal it off too. The room will still be there when spring arrives, but it won't have drained your energy in the meantime.

Adjusting Heat

Most houses are not occupied by active individuals 24/7. People sleep, go to work, run errands, and do any number of other things that don't require a warm home, so why do so many leave the heat running while they are not around to enjoy it?

One of the first things you learn with alternative heating is to mind your efficiency. A stack of firewood is a clear, finite resource that dwindles as the months go by. Start watching how you treat energy and only heat the house when necessary. Many thermostats feature programmable times to help with this.

Wearing Heavier Clothing

This might seem obvious, but houses aren't the only things that can be insulated. Sweaters, pants, and woolen socks are casual wear but enough to keep the house a few degrees colder than you could otherwise tolerate. At night, wear warm pajamas and sleep under thicker blankets. Think of heavy clothing and blankets as your own personal, portable heaters.

Space Heaters

The quickest form of alternative heating is the space heater. These typically run on electricity, gasoline, or kerosene. A space heater is cumbersome and must be carried around with its owner, and it only warms up the area immediately around it. Always be aware of safety around space heaters. They can burn skin and start fires if misused.

Space heaters serve a valuable purpose, but they are still reliant on electricity or fossil fuels and can be a major hindrance. They are a good choice in areas that only experience a few cold days a year, where the expense of a wood stove or solar system is too much to justify.

Wood Stoves

Wood stoves are a more permanent solution than space heaters and more efficient than fireplaces. They put off the same amount of heat for less fuel than the decorative hearths we are used to seeing today. Some fashionable individuals disparage them because, to be honest, they are not especially pretty. When not in use, a wood stove squats well away from the walls with a thick black pipe jutting into the ceiling.

Still, if you cared about aesthetics you wouldn't be toiling away in the dirt every day, now would you? A small wood stove should be able to reach 1000 square feet or more. Even better, a wood stove can be cooked on like a stove top. There's no need to settle for cold soup when the power goes out.

Stoves should be cleaned and inspected at least once a year to prevent clogged chimneys and potential fires. Do not leave them unattended for long periods of time while lit. Be sure to check local laws and have one professionally installed for safety's sake.

A notable alternative to the wood stove is the outdoor wood furnace, which acts like any other furnace and has significantly more range than a traditional stove because it uses existing ducts within a house.

Chopping and Storing Wood

Of course, a wood stove is useless without its titular wood. Not all firewood is created equal,, and you can't simply go outside and haul in the nearest log. The energy capacity of wood is measured in BTUs, or British Thermal Units. A good, dry hardwood such as oak makes for the best firewood. Evergreen trees are called softwoods and have a lower average BTU value. Burning pine is also inadvisable due to its high sap content, which pollutes ventilation and may start a fire in the chimney.

Most deciduous wood works well as firewood. Homesteaders with significant tree stands harvest those that fall as part of standard clean-up duty, but if you do not have that luxury you must either buy firewood, find it for free, or fell a tree yourself.

Firewood can be bought from companies or found on online classified listings. Some people give it away to anyone willing to cut it up and haul it.

When chopping down a tree, it is of paramount importance that you know what you are doing. One wrong decision could be your last or at least do significant damage to your property. People die every year after being struck by falling trees, even ones that are little more than saplings.

Use a suitable chainsaw or axe to cut a tree, sharpening it both before and after. A prime firewood candidate has a clear path to fall and is not near rocks or on a hill. Trees that are dead but not rotten are the best choice, for they require removal anyways and spend less time seasoning.

Always be aware of which direction the tree is likely to fall. If it is leaning, you won't have a choice in the matter. Otherwise, you can direct its trajectory by creating what is known as a hinge. The hinge, like one on a door, is the joint by which a falling tree turns. It helps keep the tree from twisting and dictates how it falls.

The first cut is directed along a downward slope, at around 30 degrees, at least one third the width of the tree. The second cut begins underneath it and meets it horizontally near the tree's center. A hinge should look like this, facing the way you want the tree to fall:

Be mindful of creaks and groans: They are the first warning of a falling tree. At the same time, don't rely on them, lest a quiet tree take you by surprise. You must have an escape route available at all times. Once the primary chunk has been removed, the average tree will fall on its own. If not, move to the other side of the tree and begin sawing in a horizontal line toward the open section.

The tree should begin to list before you finish. At that point, extricate the saw and start running. Leave your equipment if it is stuck. Do not head in the opposite direction, but instead at a tangent about 60 degrees from the wedge. It is not dignified, but always run, and don't bother looking back. With any luck, the tree will land where you want it, without getting entangled or otherwise derailed. If, on the other hand, the tree manages to get wedged against another, you are in for some trouble. This is an extremely dangerous situation that should only be handled by professionals with the right training. Never cut down the tree upon which the first is leaning.

Once the tree is safely down, return and begin stripping it of its branches. These can be saved for kindling. The larger branches and trunk must be divided into logs and then transported back to your home.

Stack the wood so that it has plenty of ventilation and let it dry for approximately six months before use. Wooden pallets prevent the bottom layers from rotting against the ground. A single cord of wood is 128 cubic feet of stacked logs or split wood, or approximately 5' x 5' x 5' stacked. Plan to use at least six cords per year.

Split wood to the proper size with an axe or maul on a hard, level surface. A stump works well. Have a few different sizes on hand for building the fire, ranging from narrow quarters that ignite quickly to big logs that burn all night.

Solar Heating

Wood stoves are the traditional means of heating a house, but new technology can lessen your wood consumption considerably. It's unwise, and often illegal, to rely entirely on solar power for heat and electricity, but there's no denying the convenience of a system that, once installed, can supply heat without any extra effort on your part.

Most solar heating systems heat water. That provides the energy needed for showers, laundry, washing the dishes, and other various chores. A radiant liquid system also warms floors and the air above them. Besides being very comfortable, they are more efficient by primarily heating the space that humans occupy, rather than the ceiling.

Later, generating electricity through solar panels will also be discussed.

LIVESTOCK III

It is possible for a family to live off of chickens and goats alone, but it gets awfully boring. Just like having variety in the garden is important, so too is having a decent selection of livestock. After all, if humans had been satisfied with what was available to them, why are there so many domesticated animals today?

How many and what kinds of animals you keep is up to you. A herd of cows, for example, can't be reasonably pastured on a five-acre farm. Spend some time at fairs and visiting other homesteads to learn which animals you enjoy working with. Also be sure to try their meats or other produce before making the commitment. There is nothing worse than spending thousands on livestock only to realize you can't stand them.

Meat Goats

Goats are an economical source of red meat for farms that are too small to handle cattle. A single meat goat represents less investment in time and feed than a beef cow, making losses easier to sustain and winter habitation more affordable.

Goat meat tastes like a cross between beef and venison and is cooked in much the same way as steak or ground beef.

Meat Goat Breeds

The standard meat goat is the Boer, a stocky South African breed capable of producing 75-pound kids at slaughter age. The does are fertile and excellent mothers. Boer milk is also notable for being high in butterfat, though they are less prolific than the dairy breeds.

In the United States, the Tennessee Meat Goat, or

the Fainting Goat, is another popular breed. The stiffening and contraction of the muscles of these myotonic goats improves both the texture and the size of the carcass, though the ethics of raising animals that seize up when frightened are questionable.

Raising Meat Goats

Most goats are slaughtered when they weigh 50 to 80 pounds, before the meat toughens and develops a 'bucky' flavor. A fully grown Boer buck tips the scales at about 300 pounds. Expect a carcass to yield 40 to 50 percent of the live weight.

Does are expected to give birth once a year, preferably to twins or triplets. The kids are then raised on milk and forage for as much as nine months. When given enough pasturage, this is a very economical system and results in meat at a much lower price than the feedlot-driven stuff at the store.

Slaughtering a Goat

Goats are slaughtered much like their relatives, deer. The easiest way to kill a goat is by shooting it in the head from behind, right between the ears and horns. This ends all consciousness before the animal can process what happened to it.

Suspend the goat by its hind legs and cut the

throat to bleed out the corpse. Once it is emptied, make a cut from the animal's breastbone, at the base of the neck, down the belly to the anus. Do not cut deeply enough to puncture organs; you may need to reach in and push them away from the blade. Cut around the genitals for the time being, as well as the rectum. Tie off the anus with a piece of string to keep it closed.

At this point, it's best to skin the goat. The skin should peel away easily on a fresh carcass. Cut around the head and each knee joint to remove the skin's anchor points. Begin rolling the hide off the goat, making more cuts when necessary. Once removed, you can either tan or discard it.

Open the chest and sever the windpipe and esophagus. Cut off the sexual organs and then use a hacksaw or splitter to break the pelvic bone. Carefully remove the internal organs.

You may wish to save the heart, liver, tongue, and brains to eat later. The thought makes many squeamish, but they are all nutrient-dense and were once widely served. Finally, slice off what's left of the head and legs. Removing bones from the meat is difficult and may be best left to a butcher. Divide the goat into the various cuts, much like a cow, or roast it whole on a spit. Place the meat into a refrigerator.

Sheep

Sheep are raised for their meat and distinctive wool that remains a mainstay in the fashion industry. They are also the lawn mowers of the animal kingdom, famed for clipping grass down to a manageable level and leaving fertilizer pellets behind them. Sheep can even be kept as dairy animals.

Sheep are related to goats and bear many similarities, but their divergent domestication has led to many special considerations for keeping these peculiar animals.

Sheep Breeds

Sheep are divided into two specialized categories: meat and wool, with a few dual-purpose breeds in between. Consider what it is that you want from your sheep. Do you want wool, either to sell or spin into your own fabrics? Do you want fat lambs ready to slaughter in just a few months? Do you want sheep that grow hair instead of wool, meaning you'll never need to shear them? Do you want milkers?

There are many, many breeds of sheep and even more hybrids out there. Visit a state fair or call your county extension office to find out what thrives in your region.

Merinos are perhaps the most famous wool sheep. They prefer arid regions. Generally speaking, the hotter the climate a sheep is adapted to, the finer its wool will be. Good wool sheep provide almost 15 pounds of wool per clipping.

Any medium to large breed produces robust lambs for slaughter. Suffolk or mixed-breeds are a common choice.

Housing Sheep

Unlike goats, sheep prefer grass to rough browse. They love a clean, green pasture and keep it level. When rotating pastures, an acre can hold five to seven ewes and their lambs. Plan for three or four per acre on a single pasture.

Sheep are more prone to predation than other livestock their size, due to their more docile (some say stupid) natures and the wool that sometimes creeps over their eyes. Dogs, coyotes, wolves, and wildcats all attack both lambs and adults. Lambs can even be carried away by eagles. Sheep respect fences better than goats, so your primary goal is to keep predators out.

The best fencing for sheep is a woven wire fence at least five feet high with strands of electric wire running along the top and about two feet off the ground.

As for housing, at the very least offer sheep a rough lean-to that protects them from wind, rain, and snow in the winter. Provide ample bedding: straw or shavings. Ewes also need pens for lambing season.

Call your extension office for a list of native plants poisonous to sheep, and watch the fields carefully for signs of them.

Feeding Sheep

Sheep get by on sufficient pasture but should have access to hay. Pregnant ewes appreciate grains before and after giving birth, as well as during the winter months. Sheep need access to salt licks and water at all times.

Shearing Sheep

Wool sheep must be sheared once a year, usually in spring. I recommend hiring someone to teach you the first time around, as it's not a simple process and can hurt the ewe and ruin the wool if done poorly.

Shearing is done with electric or hand clippers; buy a pair made specifically for sheep. Round up your sheep and bring one into a small pen. The pen should have a clean floor, either concrete or a tarp.

Having another person around to pin the sheep is useful. Position her on her backside, as though sitting, by holding her neck between your knees. Clip off any wool that is matted or encrusted with fecal material.

The next bit is where having a professional to demonstrate becomes invaluable. There is an art to removing fleece. Anyone can hack it off, but it takes finesse to remove it all in one piece. Work in long, smooth strokes to separate the wool from the body on one side and then spin the sheep to get the other.

If done correctly, you should be left with a continuous mound of fluffy wool ready to be sold or processed for home use. This is a good time to administer veterinary care such as shots, wormer, and trimming hooves.

Sheep and Dogs

Sheep need help staying alive. They have a tendency to blindly follow the leader, but that often leads them into more trouble than they started with. Sheep that are waterlogged drown under the weight of their own wool, and frightened ones run themselves to death or die of a fear-induced heart attack.

Of all non-poultry livestock, sheep are the most likely to meet untimely ends through one problem or another. For that reason, mankind has long enlisted the help of dogs to mind them.

The herding breeds are the smartest of all dogs.

They include the Border Collie, Australian Shepherd, and Australian Cattle Dog. These animals are fiercely intelligent, active, and work-oriented. Their natural prey drive has been channeled into a less violent path, and they are quick to take cues, learn commands, and anticipate the moves of their flock.

Livestock guardian dogs mingle with the herd or patrol an established perimeter. They are raised with their herd and learn to consider them as family. The Great Pyrenees was bred to blend in with sheep and is one of the easier LGDs to own. Despite prevailing folk-wisdom, socialize LGD puppies to prevent bites and fearful aggression down the road.

Raising Slaughter Lambs

Lambs are slaughtered at around six months of age. Anything older than a year is mutton. If you think you don't like the taste of lamb, make sure you have tried real grass-fed meat before writing it off. Like cows, more and more lambs are being finished on grain rather than the traditional pasturage and, again like cows, the end result cannot compare.

Lamb and mutton are red meats, similar to goat and beef. They are served on many religious holidays, particularly Easter in the United States. Sheep are slaughtered much like goats.

Pigs

Pigs have a bad reputation as lazy, smelly, and greedy creatures. In fact, they are a tidy and intelligent animal and a welcome part of many farms.

Pigs are the garbage disposals of the homestead. They can and will eat nearly anything from every food group. Extra milk, fruit peels, expired vegetables, and even old meat are happily downed by pigs, which turn those excess nutrients into delicious pork. They are prolific breeders, and a single sow produces more meat than the typical family can eat. Usually the unwanted piglets, or shoats, are sold off after weaning.

Pig Breeds

There are many pig breeds, but you are best served looking for whatever is available locally. All but the extreme show breeds provide ample meat. Hybrids perform better than either parent, but shouldn't be purchased if you plan to breed your own hogs.

Housing Pigs

Pigs also have a reputation for loving the mud. They have limited sweat glands, so they use the cool dirt to regulate their temperature. All pigs should have a wallow to go to as needed. They also need shelter, much like goats and sheep. A stable is preferred, but a lean-to should be enough to take care of them. Market-weight pigs need at least 10 square feet of shelter each.

Pigs do well on pasture, and ample space is the only way to reduce the odor of an omnivorous digestive tract similar to our own. They are strong and crafty and dig under fences if they can. A woven-wire fence will hold them, as will electric strands. To keep pigs sustainably on a pasture, place no more than five per acre. This number rises to about 10 when rotating.

Feeding Pigs

Even pastured pigs need some help to grow more than a pound a day. Premixed feeds are best bought from feed mills, in bulk, to handle the demands of these ultimate meat animals. Weaned pigs start at the highest concentrations of protein, which are slowly lowered until slaughtered.

Pigs eat almost any waste, but be aware that they are omnivorous. It's unwise to keep chickens and other small animals in the same pen, and practice safety around a group of hogs. They have eaten their owners before and will do it again.

Pigs are used in many health studies because of their bodies' similarities to our own, including their capacity to harbor communicable diseases. With that in mind, anything that could make you sick yourself shouldn't be on a pig's menu.

Raising Pigs

A sow has two litters per year and gives birth to about 12 piglets each time. Those piglets are slaughtered at six months when they weigh approximately 250 pounds. That results in about 125 pounds of cuts, meaning the average sow is responsible for 3000 pounds of finished meat every year.

Slaughter a pig as you would any other medium-sized mammal.

Cattle

Cows (more appropriately "cattle") are the ultimate livestock, so long as you have the resources for them. They require plenty of land and copious amounts of feed, and their size makes them a hazard to work with. In exchange, farmers have a ready supply of more milk and beef than they could ever consume on their own.

Whether you choose to raise cows depends on your acreage and your dedication to grass-fed beef and dairy.

Cow Breeds

Cows are divided into beef and dairy breeds, though some are kept for both. Dairy cows are docile and bred to produce the most milk per pound of feed possible. Jerseys, Holsteins and Guernseys are all traditional choices. Beef cows are more independent, larger, and grow more muscle. Angus and Hereford are some of the more popular beef breeds. In between are the dual-purpose cattle such as the Brown Swiss.

One breed is gaining a wider reputation among small farmers as an economical cow for the homestead. Dexter cattle are miniature cows weighing between 600 and 1100 pounds. They are good for both meat and milk and use significantly less feed and land per head than their larger relatives.

Housing Cows

Because of their weight, cattle housing must be sturdier than that of smaller livestock. Anything flimsy or unsecured gets pushed over quickly. Use thick posts and timber or buy a metal-and-plastic shelter for them. A three-sided lean-to is often used with 30 square feet per cow.

Dairy operations should have a milking area as well. In large dairies, that is a separate barn with automated milking equipment, but for the smaller farm it need only be a spacious area with clean, concrete floors and room to escape a kicking cow.

The number of cows to place in a pasture is nearly impossible to recommend. Depending on grass quality, you may be able to keep a mother and her calf on one acre or it might take three. Start at a ratio of one cow per 2.5 acres before adjusting accordingly. Cows are contained with electric, barbed, or woven-wire fencing.

Feeding Cows

Cows graze grass on pasture and largely support themselves if given enough room. In the winter, however, plan to feed them at least 30 pounds of hay per head every day. This accounts for waste and should leave enough in case of unseasonably long winters. The cost of overwintering a cow can be substantial. Check hay prices in your area and compare it to the number of days in your climate's winter to get an estimate.

Silage is fermented corn that improves nutrient absorption and is fed as a supplement to hay. The amount fed per day depends on hay consumption.

Raising Cows

Always be cautious around cows. They are large and won't hesitate to barrel into you if they feel pressured. Never place yourself between a cow and a wall or fence in cramped conditions.

A dairy cow must be milked twice a day for her own comfort and can be expected to give several gallons of milk each time. Milking by hand follows a similar procedure as with goats, only in a lot more volume.

Slaughtering sheep, goats, and pigs is easy to do at home because of their relatively small size. A cow, on the other hand, weighs thousands of pounds and needs heavier equipment, including a meat saw and a front-end loader for a tractor.

A grass-fed cow is usually ready to eat at 24 to 30 months, while a grain-finished one is done at 15 to 18. The old strategy of 'shooting between the eyes' doesn't work for cows. Instead, aim higher, almost directly between the ears. Cut the throat as soon as it hits the ground and begin by removing the testicles, lower front legs, and head.

After the initial cleaning, suspend the cow and begin the same process used for other animals. It helps to split the carcass. Age beef in a clean area for about a week before bringing it indoors and freezing.

It may be easier to take the cows to a certified processor or enlist the services of a mobile butcher rather than deal with the process of dressing out such a huge animal, but it is good to practice at least once.

Bees

In the last few years, the native bee population of North America has taken a staggering blow as the result of colony collapse disorder. Pollinators are scarce in many parts of the United States, leaving farmers bereft of their oldest and most valuable allies.

Keeping bees not only fertilizes your trees and vegetables, but it also supplies honey every year with little daily care required. Every homestead should have at least one hive.

Bees are marvelous creatures, and not just from a utilitarian point of view. They have rigid social structures, advanced communication methods, and sophisticated engineering, even though each individual's brain is about the size of a seed from your garden. They are the ultimate illustration of teamwork overcoming the limitations of a single organism. Survivalists and homesteaders can learn many lessons from them.

Of course, before buying bees, ensure that you and everyone in the household are not allergic to their stings. They can be fatal, so go into a medical clinic to be tested before handling any insects.

Bees aren't difficult to keep, but it can be tricky to make them produce. If at all possible, take a beekeeping course and enlist the help of an expert. This is not just fattening up a pig: this is managing your own small civilization, and there are different kinds of buildings to recognize, the important members of society to memorize, and learning what conditions will lead to a rich harvest.

Bee Housing

Check local ordinances before installing beehives. These bugs are not always welcome neighbors. Set them away from heavily trafficked areas because, to be fair, they are not particularly fond of neighbors either.

Bee hives can be purchased new or used, but be aware that some states require testing used equipment. A bee hive kit is inexpensive and fairly easy to put together, and it also gives you an in-depth look at how hives are set up. Place them in a sunny spot and don't overcrowd. Start with one hive and establish new ones as your population grows.

Most hives are built as a vertical structure with several layers called "supers." The top is a covered door for easy access by the beekeeper, which leads down into the honey super. Underneath that is the brood chamber, where larvae are fed and raised in dense honeycombs.

The honey supers are the layers you need to worry about most. In fat years, add more to give the bees adequate storage space. Honey is stored in honeycombs- the familiar hexagons of beeswax. Bees build these instinctively, but a foundation of started shapes speeds the process up. Save the wax from the honeycombs after removal, or place them back in the hive to give the bees a head start next year.

Clean out and repair hives once a year. It may eventually become necessary to transfer an active colony into a new hive as natural wear and tear runs the old one down.

Feeding Bees

Bees fly miles around the hive in search of pollen to bring back to the colony. They love fruit blossoms in particular, but almost any will do.

The flavor of a hive's honey depends on the pollen the workers collect. For example, bees that spend the majority of their time in an apple orchard produce honey that is quite different from a hive that buzzes through wildflowers. Bees that are left to their own devices typically produce darker, richer honey than the stuff found in stores, which is often cultivated from clover pollen.

Sometimes, however, a flower creates terrible honey. Azaleas and mountain laurels have a reputation for producing toxic honey, though bees largely ignore them. Other plants produce honey that just plain tastes bad. Control the plants on your property and give the bees plenty of tastier alternatives to work with. Many farmers plant a patch of clover to entice both deer and the resident bee populations.

Pesticides used on your property or within a few miles will kill any bees that fall foul of it. This may be a problem if you are situated next to a commercial farm, but many neighbors are amenable to cutting down on their use of chemicals, especially if you offer them a share of the honey.

During the winter, bees live off of their honey and pollen stores. The colder Northern states need at least 75 pounds of honey per hive. This is disappointing to beekeepers, of course, but it's essential for the survival of the colony. Bees do not hibernate, so they must be kept fed all through the cold months.

In late summer or fall, bees begin moving their honey deeper into the hive, to the brooding chamber where they will spend the winter huddled together. Always check that these levels have a good supply of honey before removing some for personal use.

If your bees begin to run low, buy pollen cakes and place them within the hive, or provide solid sugar. Check beginning in mid-winter and into early spring.

Bees also need access to water near the hive like any other animal. It should be clean and preferably running to slow the transmission of disease.

Buying Bees

Nowadays, you can buy a package of bees online and have it shipped right to your home. To spare them the rigors of shipping, however, it's better to get your bees from a proven beekeeper with disease-free stock. This also gives you a local contact to help you get started and go to with problems.

There are three "classes" of bees. The queen is the heart of the hive. She lays thousands of eggs every day and each worker in the colony is her daughter. Workers are the ones that fly out to collect pollen, cultivate it into honey, tend to the queen, and feed the new generations. The drone is the male bee. His only purpose is to supply genetic material to the queen.

Introducing bees to an empty hive is relatively simple, and they are unlikely to be aggressive in the first uncertain stages. Some recommend shaking them out of the box and into the hive, while others choose to let them crawl out on their own. The hive should have full sugar feeders to keep them happy and willing to settle down.

Unless you purchase an established hive, the workers will probably be unfamiliar with the queen. If they are not acclimated to each other, they may harm her. Some sellers pack the queen into a small cage that can only be opened after the bees have chewed away a block of sugar. This time-delay system keeps the queen safe as the workers learn her scent.

Handling Bees

Most people have experienced a bee sting at one point or another, but few go out of their way to intrude upon an entire hive. The risk is well worth the reward, however, so long as you have the right equipment and know-how.

The standard beekeeper's outfit looks something like an astronaut's, and it serves much the same function of shielding the entire body from harm. Where a space suit keeps air in, however, a beekeeper's uniform keeps bees out. A hat with a veil, thick coveralls, gloves, and pant legs sealed to the boots are all needed to prevent bees crawling through a narrow opening and onto bare flesh.

Sedate bees during invasive procedures with a smoker. This puts them into a groggy state without doing any permanent harm. A hive tool is a long, crow-bar like piece of metal or plastic used to pry the different layers apart.

Diseases and Pests

Bees are prone to diseases and must be monitored closely. Stay familiar with what's going through the area. At this point I sound like a broken record, but the local extension office will be able to help and refer you to an apiary inspector.

Keep bees safe by limiting exposure to other colonies and using only new or tested equipment. If you give combs back to the workers to refill, throw them out every two years. Buy bees from trustworthy sources to avoid being saddled with contaminated stock from the start.

Some diseases attack eggs and larvae, while others strike adults. Fungi and bacteria infiltrate the brooding chamber and corrupt eggs before they can hatch, leaving nothing but a mess behind. The worst of them is American Foulbrood, a bacterial infection which kills larvae. The clearest sign of it is a dark and concave cap over the diseased cell, as well as gooey, ropey dead larvae inside. It is treated with antibiotics, though not cured. To purge it completely, the hive must be burned.

There are several other common diseases, but the big concern is mites. *Varroa jacobsoni* are Indian mites fatal to the standard bees used in America. They are small, brown creatures with eight legs that cling to the bees. They can wipe out a colony within a year, but are drastically reduced or eliminated with special pesticide strips.

Check hives at least twice a month to monitor bees for signs of disease or pests. The faster a problem is caught, the less likely it is to destroy your bees and halt the honey crop.

Propagating

In spring, a full hive starts to feel a bit cramped, and your queen may begin hatching out younger versions of herself. Since no hive needs two queens, the youngster, when she grows old enough, departs the hive with an escort of workers to found a new colony.

You can choose to guide the swarm into another hive, let them go, or destroy queen cells before they hatch.

Swarming bees are more docile than their established counterparts and almost never sting. They cluster on branches and other surfaces and can be gently shaken or brushed into a new hive, if desired.

Honey

Bees are worth their upkeep for their pollinating efforts alone, but honey is just as remarkable as its creators. It is a natural sweetener that stores for thousands of years under the right conditions.

Plan to use about seven gallons of honey per year for a family of four- approximately three hives' worth. Always have more hives than you think you'll need, because things have a way of going wrong and bees are reliant on their own stores to get them through winter.

Leave at least 75 pounds of honey for the bees, preferably 100 in cold climates. The rest is free for your family to enjoy. Harvest in the fall, after the collecting seasons are over. Smoke the hive and remove the excess supers. The combs are covered in a layer of wax.

At this time, you may want to remove and save the propolis, a resinous substance bees use to fill in small gaps in the hive. It has a number of interesting properties and is said to be beneficial to human health.

Begin extracting the honey by uncapping the cells. This is usually done with a heated or electric knife. The wax should peel off, exposing the honey beneath. Keep the wax to seperate clinging honey or use later in various crafts.

Next, the honey is extracted from the comb via centrifugal force, unless you are comfortable eating the comb. Small mechanical extractors made for hobbyists are common nowadays, and it's not difficult to pick one up at a fair price. The honey is then strained and the wax either placed back in the hive or processed for use in other projects. Store honey in a clean jar. It does not need to be canned or frozen.

Unorthodox Livestock

Besides the familiar animals that have been raised on American farms for centuries, there are also a few others that are worthy of a brief mention.

Alpacas and Llamas

These South American camelids were domesticated thousands of years ago and are still widely kept today. Llamas are larger and more suited for meat production and carrying burdens, while alpacas are best known for their rich fibers. They are often kept with sheep or goats and are reputed to be good guardians.

Emus and Ostriches

For a while, emus and ostriches were a big fad in the farming community. These monstrous birds carry the most nutritious and low-fat red meat on the market, and for almost a decade they were hailed as the next beef.

Of course, most Americans didn't like the idea of eating such an unconventional meat, and there was never really a strong demand for it. Today both birds are expensive and rare in the United States, but if you manage to get your hands on a breeding pair you're in for some excellent dinners.

These species are not particularly domesticated and can be dangerous to handle thanks to their size and power. An ostrich can kill with a single kick.

Fish

Once upon a time, fish were cheap and plentiful. Now, however, the oceans are emptying and most fish sold in stores come from farms. If others can raise them, why can't you?

Fish are easy keepers. They need a suitable pond with proper filtering and cleaning systems, but if given enough food and the right environment they flourish. Catfish and tilapia are two common choices thanks to their fast growth and ability to survive in stagnant water.

Of the unorthodox livestock, fish are probably the best investment.

MAKING BASIC SUPPLIES

For the most part, the first three years on a farm should be about learning how to collect raw materials. Considering how much can go wrong with even the most basic of tasks, it's almost necessary to put everything else on hold as you build experience.

By your fourth year at this, however, you should have a good command of gardening and be increasingly familiar with raising livestock. Once you have everything outside running smoothly, it's time to turn to your home.

Some homesteaders make everything in this chapter, and some make none. There is no denying that homespun and sewn clothes may look a bit old-fashioned in town, for example, and it takes much less time to just go to the store and buy them. Nevertheless, they are good skills to have.

Candles

Candles are an alternative to electricity when you only need low lighting and are also useful during power outages. They are made with a support substance, wicks, dyes, and scents.

The support can be beeswax, tallow, or wax produced by the bayberry family. There are also certain materials that, realistically, can only be bought from the store, including soy wax and paraffin. Use what you have. Beeswax is preferred, but the argument against taking too much wax from a hive has already been made in the previous livestock chapter.

Wicks are the strand that provides fuel for the fire. Melted wax "wicks" up the rope, giving the fire something to burn. Cotton is the common material for this. The thickness of the wick determines the size of the candle. Thicker wicks burn larger and faster. The two, flame and support, must move together, lest the flame be drowned or starved.

Creating a candle is not difficult and lends itself well to creativity. Most are made by pouring the wax or tallow into a mold and suspending the wick in it. Once the wax has set, the wick is cut down to its proper level and the candle removed from the mold. Experiment with colors and scents (crayons are great for color, but not for scent,) to find what you like.

Cleaning

Believe it or not, households were kept clean before the invention of modern chemical mixes. Certainly there were a few more smells and stains, but they were a natural part of life, rather than disgusting and a sign of poor housekeeping.

The cleaning recipes of a century ago were simple. Instead of a cocktail of smells, dyes, and a hundred different molecules, most families used a single agent such as bleach or baking soda. They are still readily available to this day, though often overlooked in favor of sleek packaging and lemon-scented reassurance.

This can be seen everywhere; we douse ourselves in manufactured compounds without a second thought, because we have been raised to do so. Then word gets out about yet another recall or a new carcinogen, we check our labels, and go right back to applying products directly to our skin and surfaces.

The damage doesn't stop there. Everything gets flushed down a drain, from hellish toilet cleaners to shampoo. That water has to go somewhere and leeches into the soil, causing a harmful build-up of toxins that destroys habitats and farmlands.

By your fourth year on a farm, there is no question that you will be used to a little more mess than most. Cut your dependence on antibacterial soaps and the ridiculous products we use in the name of a 10-percent-shinier shine. There is controlling germs, and then there's killing the environment in the name of living in a catalog.

The solutions here have the added benefit of being both cheaper and often healthier than their counterparts at the store.

Ammonia

Ammonia is the primary ingredient in many cleaning solutions. It is used to clean up greasy deposits and as a disinfectant. Dilute pure ammonium hydroxide to a 10 percent solution. Be careful when using this chemical. It turns into ammonia gas when exposed to the air, and too much causes irritation of the skin and eyes or even poisoning. Open up your windows and doors when cleaning with ammonia.

Most importantly, never mix ammonia with chlorine bleach. The two chemicals combine to form a toxic gas that could land you in the hospital.

Baking Soda

Baking soda, or sodium bicarbonate, is one of the most useful compounds available in the home. It whitens stains, eliminates odors, and serves as an abrasive for scrubbing. It even makes a safe tooth whitener when used in moderation. If something's gone wrong indoors, putting baking soda on it usually helps.

Bleach

Bleach is a controversial tool for the eco-conscious. When washed down the drain it damages the environment and may release carcinogens into the water supply. On the other hand, it is also a powerful disinfectant. Minimal bleach use is probably unavoidable, but should be kept as infrequent as possible.

Never mix bleach with another chemical. It has a tendency to form toxic and even fatal gases when exposed to the wrong molecules.

Citric Acid

Citric acid, the 'tart' taste in lemon and lime juices, is a great alternative to bleach. It whitens and kills bacteria, making it the perfect solution to clean toilets and other white surfaces. Give it a try and you might swear off pricey toilet cleaners forever.

Soap

No cleaning section would be complete without soap. In fact, further on you'll learn how to make it yourself. Traditional soaps are made with lye and fat and contain no manufactured chemicals. Use bar soap to wash yourself and flakes for laundry and dishes.

Vinegar

Vinegar rivals baking soda as an all-around handy chemical. It degreases, deodorizes, whitens, and is a virulent anti-fungal solution. In fact, apple cider vinegar is often mixed into livestock's water supply as a harmless health supplement or treatment for fungal diseases, and it is sprayed on fruit trees for the same reason. White distilled vinegar is a better choice for home jobs.

Clothing

This is one section that I personally do not practice. In my opinion, making clothing is one of those things that takes too long for the results. However, learning to spin yarn and knit or sew fabrics can be a rewarding hobby and clothe a family on the cheap.

This quick guide details the steps to turn wool fresh off a sheep's back into yarn, as well as how to transform cloth and string into presentable outfits.

Processing Wool

Once the wool is off the sheep, it must be washed and trimmed for cleanliness. Start by dunking the fleece in 140-degree water with a squirt of dish detergent in it, and then submerge it in cold to remove the oil. It may take several long soaks to work everything out. Scouring is faster when using an acid bath. Cut off any wool marred by manure and other undesirable materials.

The fleece is then allowed to dry, preferably through natural air drying. The next step is to card the wool- making it uniform and more manageable, either mechanically or by hand. Carding drums small enough for a home spinner are available, otherwise use hand carders, which resemble two fine brushes. The fleece is rolled between the two surfaces or brushes until it is all aligned in the same direction.

Next, the wool is spun. This might be done on a machine or an old-fashioned spinning-wheel. There are a thousand different spinning methods and techniques, and each spinner seems to think that his or her way is the best of them all. In the end, the wool is pulled tight and wound together to form the yarn everyone's grandmother seemed to have lying around.

Knitting and Crocheting

Knitting is the most common means of turning yarn into clothing, but there's also crochet, which uses a different set of movements and apparatus.

I said earlier that I forego making my own clothes, but everyone should know how to knit a sweater, scarf, hat, and gloves. Knitting uses two needles to hold and guide yarn into a series of stitches, or loops, which form a larger coherent pattern. Well-made knitwear is every bit as warm and functional as the same item from a store, and much cheaper.

Crochet uses only one tool, a hook, and has a different notation than knitting. Crochet usually results in more delicate, detail-oriented work, such as tablecloths or shawls. Consider crochet for when you need lighter clothing or simply want a break from knitting.

Working with threads is the best way for a small farmer to transform the wool from his or her sheep into a practical resource. Even better, it's becoming a more and more sociable hobby. Look around your area for knitting clubs to get started.

Cottons

Making cloth from raw cotton is a more difficult proposition. The threads are much finer and usually woven into a single sheet. It is possible to process raw cotton into yarn, which is knitted or crocheted like wool.

If you buy fabrics from a store, you can create more modern-looking clothing. Sewing is another skill everyone should know, but few schools still teach it. Start with the basics by making a decent stitch, then a line of stitches, and then an attractive union of two fabrics. From there, practice cutting and sewing various patterns until you are able to make shirts, pants, and anything else you desire. Cottons are best for summer, when woolen knits may be too heavy to wear comfortably.

Lotions

Lotion, like soap, is a cosmetic product applied directly to the skin. It is an ancient part of beauty regimens and fills the practical purpose of moisturizing skin. Just like soap, though, lotion has been transformed into a cocktail indecipherable to anyone lacking a degree in chemistry.

Lotion is quick to make and uses ingredients you may have on the farm already. Lanolin, for example, is a natural by-product of wool and a valuable component of lotion. Usually an oil, such as olive oil, is added, along with beeswax, aloe vera, and any other scent or dye you prefer.

Shorter-lived ingredients like goat's milk have a limited storage time but are also very rejuvenating. Mix the ingredients together slowly, in a blender or by hand. Once the lotion has set, store it in a jar in the fridge to extend its viable period.

Quilting

Once you know how to sew, you'll never run out of projects. Quilting is at once an art form and a way to stay warm at night. It is the combination of different fabrics, joined together to create an insulating effect as well as beautiful patterns.

Most quilts have three layers: the back, the batting, and the top. The back and batting are usually broad sheets of cloth, while the top may be any number of different fabrics. Accuracy is essential when planning, cutting, and sewing the top. A fraction of an inch here and a wrinkle there will bring the whole quilt out of alignment further down the road. Start with a single sheet for the top and then progress to simple squares. Once you get the hang of it you can move on to advanced quilts.

Soap

Soap should technically be listed under cleaning products, but it's so useful that it warrants its own section. There's a misconception that homemade soaps are harsh and damaging. That is the result of using too much lye and is avoidable.

There are a few limitations to their usage, however. For example, washing items in cold water doesn't work well, and hard water will leave a sticky ring around the container.

Lye

First and foremost, lye is dangerous to handle and burns exposed skin. That doesn't sound like a great ingredient for a skin-care product, but in small quantities it is a powerful cleaning agent. Always wear safety gloves and glasses along with long clothing. Lye can be neutralized with vinegar in an emergency.

Purchase lye or make your own. It is sold as the chemical compound $NaOH$, or sodium hydroxide. Home-made lye is typically potassium hydroxide. To make it from scratch, gather up wood ashes from a stove or small burner. Hardwoods are the best for this. Also collect soft water from a rain barrel.

Drill small holes in the bottom of a wooden barrel and set a sterile container underneath it to catch the dripping lye. Be sure the barrel is stable over the container! Place clean rocks at the bottom of the barrel and cover them with straw. Then fill up the rest with ash.

Pour the rain water into the barrel slowly. The water that drips out contains lye. Continue pouring that lye water through the barrel until you can float an egg in it with a quarter-sized patch remaining above the surface. At that point, the lye is concentrated enough to use for soap-making.

Mixing Soap

Lye gives soap its cleaning properties, and everything else is just a bonus. Coconut, olive, and castor oil create creamy, lathery soaps like the bars we are used to today, but any sort of fat or oil can be used, including sunflower oil and lard. Goat's milk also makes an especially fine soap, but doesn't last as long as soaps made from lard or other more stable fats. Use what you have.

When not following an established recipe, it is critical that you calculate the correct amount of lye. Too much will burn your skin and parch your hair, but too little makes the soap nothing more than a glorified lotion. There are several calculators online to help with this.[19]

If all of the items covered here sound too difficult or time-consuming, give them a try before you write them off. Your health is the only thing you have, when it comes down to it, and removing yourself from the world of pre-packaged carcinogens is well worth spending two or three hours a week making your own household supplies.

YEAR FIVE

GARDENING V

Whether or not you follow this chapter depends on your commitment to self-sufficiency and how much space you have left on your property. Back in the introduction to this book I attempted to draw a distinction between "real" self-sufficiency and a modernized version of it. The gardening covered now falls more into the former camp.

Picture for a moment the ubiquitous food pyramid (though in recent years the powers-that-be have changed its design.) At the top are the sweets and fats. If you raise bees or fruits or keep the skin on your chicken carcasses, you are producing that food group. Beneath it are the meats and dairies, both in ready supply for anyone keeping cows, goats, or other livestock. After that are fruits and vegetables, which you should have in spades.

The bottom, and the largest portion, of the pyramid, however, has been under-represented so far in this book. Many of the plants covered in prior gardening chapters, especially corn, provide carbohydrates, but not the grains we are used to.

People use wheat, oats, and rye for baking, most notably bread. They store well and make an excellent addition to any winter pantry. And, because they are near the bottom of the food chain and stuffed with carbs, grains are some of the most efficient energy sources you can grow.

The Latter Day Saints' Preparedness Manual recommends at least 400 pounds of grain per man per year, or about 1500 for a family of four.[20] The majority of that will be wheat and corn.

Livestock, however, tend to be the biggest source of grain consumption on a farm, and it's with them in mind that you should determine how much to plant.

A substantial amount of planted grasses and grains beg for heavy machinery, namely a tractor with harvesting and tilling attachments. The alternative, working fields by hand, is a big undertaking when planting more than an acre. If you are thrifty and patient, you can pick up the required machinery for a few thousand dollars. Harvesting manually costs only one or two hundred dollars, by comparison.

Planting Grasses and Grains

To clarify, the concept of growing grains and grasses is divided over two different sections in this chapter. The gardening part addresses how to grow and harvest them and how much to plant for a single person. Growing for livestock feed is explored more thoroughly later.

Barley

Barley is a cereal grain beloved to home brewers. It is not an optimal flour for bread-making on its own, but when combined with wheat flour it gives bread a delicious, unique flavor. It is also fermented into alcohol, served in soups, and highly nutritious for livestock.

Barley is usually sold without its husk and with most of its nutrients polished away. The husk is a common trait of many grains, but barley's is attached strongly. It is removed through light toasting before being run through a grinder. The more polished, "pearl" barley stores better but has fewer nutrients. Barley can be purchased in either spring or winter varieties, and there are now hull-less types available.

One bushel, or 48 pounds, of barley requires about 1000 square feet. Work the soil beforehand and broadcast the seeds before covering them with a light layer of soil. Scattering the seeds by hand and raking over them will suffice if you don't have larger equipment. Plan for about 1,000,000 plants and 100 pounds of seed per acre.[21]

Harvest barley once it is dry enough that the kernels snap rather than bend, after about 60 days. Harvest with a combine or by hand. To manually collect it, use a sharp knife or a scythe equipped with a cradle to cut the stalks about one foot from the top. Lay the barley heads facing the same direction and bind them into "sheaves."

Thresh barley by beating the sheaves against a surface, such as into a metal can or plastic storage bucket. The grains should dislodge themselves. Grind the barley as necessary and then store it in a dry, secure area. Pearl barley lasts about a year, husked considerably less.

Dent Corn

Corn was introduced back in year two, and growing it on a larger scale uses most of the same concepts elaborated upon there. This, however, is feed corn, otherwise known as dent corn. Industrial farms are managing 300 or more bushels at 56 pounds each per acre, but on the homestead you are more likely to average about 100. Plan to have about 500 square feet per bushel.[7]

Plant corn in rows two or three feet apart. Assume a 25 percent germination rate. Till or mow between the rows to keep weeds down. Thin corn sprouts to one foot spacing.

Corn is a heavy feeder and needs plenty of nutrients to stay healthy. Rotate crops out with legumes to help build up the soil and prevent the accumulation of diseases and pests.

Unlike sweet corn, dent corn must dry out before harvest. If you have planted less than an acre, picking by hand is easy with a truck for hauling. There are a few manual tools for removing the husk and kernels in large quantities, otherwise you'll end up with some blistered fingers without the right machinery. Store corn in a safe location. If dried, it should last two or three years.

Hay

Hay is a staple for many animals, including cattle, goats, sheep, and rabbits. Even better, it's made up in part by legumes, which release valuable nitrogen into the soil.

There are two types of hay: grass and legume. Legume hay such as alfalfa is higher in protein but it may be too energy-dense, while grass hay is easier to grow but usually needs grains as a supplement.

Don't get too intimidated by hay. It's exactly the same concept as putting away fruits and vegetables for the winter, only adapted to the needs of animals. If the grass isn't toxic, it probably won't hurt as a hay (though high protein levels can be harmful.) For the first year, try 1/3 legume and 2/3 grass seed and supplement with grains as needed. From there, tweak your formula as you see fit.

If you don't have heavy equipment, harvest hay with a scythe on a sunny day when there's no forecasted rain. Cut the hay and let it dry in the sun for a few days, until it snaps easily. Rain is disastrous during this period and ruins the crop. Be sure it is dry, however, before bringing it in. Moist hay composts and becomes so hot that it can burn down a whole barn.

Once dried, consider renting a baler or paying a neighbor to come by with one. Otherwise, collect it loose and move it to a dry and secure storage area.

Oats

Oats make great straw, oatmeal, and feed and are packed with proteins. Like barley, oats have a hard hull, making them a royal pain for anyone without access to industrial equipment. There are hull-less varieties available, but they suffer from poorer performance.

Expect about 80 bushels per acre, or approximately one bushel per 500 square feet.[22] They like the cold and plenty of water. Sow the seeds as you would barley. Oats are harvested once the plant begins to brown and the kernels, when squeezed, no longer give off a milky fluid but are still soft. Cut the heads from the stalks and allow them to dry in a safe, well-ventilated place. Hull by heating and milling.

Soybeans

Soybeans are neither grass nor grain, but I include them here because they are a key ingredient in animal feed. They have exploded in popularity recently as a healthy wonder-food- a high-protein bean that's easy to grow and good for the body in a number of ways. Whether or not that's entirely accurate is best left to the scientists.

Putting aside human health, soybeans are the primary reason our meat is so cheap. There is no better source of carbohydrates and protein to fatten up a cow, pig, or chicken quickly. On the other hand, it has become just another GMO plant grown in huge swaths across the country, requiring massive amounts of chemicals to stay alive. With that in mind, it is more responsible to grow at least some of your own.

Soybeans are planted and raised like the bush beans discussed in year four. They like a long, hot growing season. For human consumption, pick them while the beans are still green and tender and fill out their pods. Beans used for feed remain on the stalk until they are dry and yellow. Expect 20 to 40 bushels per acre.

Wheat

If you grow anything in this section, grow wheat. Everyone loves wheat, save a few people with unfortunate allergies. There are winter varieties harvested in early summer and spring varieties that mature in fall. You can buy soft and hard wheat as well, both red and white. Hard wheat does best in cold climates and have higher protein, the soft in warm. Red wheat has red bran and a slightly bitter flavor, whereas white wheat lacks the phenolic acid and tannin that gives the bran its hue. A hard red wheat is best for bread-making.

Start by sowing 100lbs of seed per acre. Work the land before broadcasting and cover it over with a rake, about 1" to 2". Expect around 40 bushels per acre at 60 pounds a bushel. [7]

Wheat is a hardy, happy grower. Once the stalks turn golden and the kernels become dry and crispy, they are ready to harvest. If you are harvesting by hand, do it while the grains are still able to be dented with a fingernail. Harvest with a scythe and cradle, bundle, dry, thresh, and store. At this point you can grind it into flour, add it to feed, or whatever else you desire. The stalks make excellent straw. Wheat stores for years if kept dry.

ALTERNATIVE ENERGY III

At the very start of this book, I listed the four things every human needs to survive: water, food, shelter, and energy. I recommended that your first four years of homesteading be dedicated primarily to gathering water and food, assuming you already had housing and energy.

Year five, however, is when you should begin thinking about this as a lifestyle rather than a demanding hobby. Now that you have a solid foundation for survival, you can turn to your creature comforts.

This is not the first time this guide has discussed energy. Year two focused on emergency situations and, more importantly, reducing daily electricity consumption. Year three discussed new ways to heat a home, including through solar power. Both were meant to lay the groundwork for year five, which advises dramatic changes that will be made easier with a healthy attitude toward electricity use.

I'll admit to my own love for electricity readily. What I don't love is being beholden to the electric company's infrastructure. Some homesteaders follow the Luddite tradition and shed as many trappings of modern society as possible. That's an admirable pursuit, but it's not for everyone. Given today's society and the near impossibility of functioning in it without electricity, the best solution is a compromise by cutting down energy use and switching to renewable resources.

Alternative energy has been the recipient of extensive research and development over the past decade and has become more efficient than ever. At this point, a solar or wind system represents a significant investment that should pay for itself over time and may be offset by government incentives.

Many local laws require that homes remain connected to the power grid. Is it right? Perhaps not, but, like everything in this book, be sure to check that you are not opening yourself up to a host of legal issues before acting on anything.

Solar

Solar energy is the most recognized type of alternative energy, and for good reason. It is the direct harvest of the Earth's greatest energy source: the sun. Farmers have done this for years, though their tools were plants and animals. Modern technology has boosted the efficiency of collection considerably through solar panels (but we still use the plants and animals!)

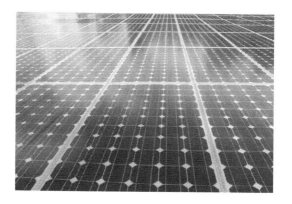

Solar energy has already been mentioned in terms of heating, but photovoltaic systems use a different process to turn the sun's rays into electricity. Basically, the energy entering a solar cell is converted into an electric current, which can then be channeled into appliances as needed.

There are storage systems available for nights and prolonged periods of gloom, usually chargeable batteries, but sole use of a solar system lends credence to the old motto, "early to bed, early to rise."

Professionally installing a photovoltaic system on a home with low-to-medium power consumption costs about $10,000 but can be as much as $30,000. There are DIY project plans available that reduce the cost to less than $5,000, if you have the technical skills and ambition.

Wind

Most places worth farming see plenty of sunlight and are perfect for a solar system. Wind power carries no such guarantee but has been a staple of farms for centuries. Windmills pumped water to fields, livestock, and homes, saving countless man-hours in the process. You might even want to implement this primitive system as a backup measure on your own homestead.

Now, windmills also generate electricity. Whether or not they are worth the cost of installation, however, depends upon your climate. High hilltops that see frequent, sustained winds are prime candidates. Places that see a few gusts a day are not.

The other big problem with wind turbines is that, even when they are operating profitably and supplying real energy to a home, they are still moving machines, and moving machines break. Repairs on high towers are dangerous and expensive.

In short, wind technology is a promising field, especially in large-scale operations that have thousands of acres and trained professionals at their disposal. As of 2012, however, the technology for home use just isn't at a point that I would broadly endorse it. Look into it for your particular circumstances, but if you have to pick only one form of alternative energy, go with solar.

LIVESTOCK IV

Prior to this, every chapter dealing with new livestock has covered how to buy, raise, and utilize them. As you build established populations of good breeding stock, though, you will want to continue the lines through your own husbandry. There is also the question of sustaining animals so that they consume minimal purchased resources.

This final chapter on livestock is devoted to settling in for the long haul with the creatures who will supply most of your proteins in the future. If managed poorly, they become a drain on finances and more trouble than they are worth, but with the right handling they will keep your family fed and prosperous for years to come.

Keep experimenting with new breeds and species to learn which work best for your farm's dynamics. Some people can't stand working with goats but love keeping sheep, or vice-versa. You may find a new passion breeding royal pigs or cultivate a race of barnyard mutts that churn out more meat for every pound of feed than any established breed. There are very few hard and fast rules when it comes to keeping animals, and you will discover what you like as time goes on.

Animal Husbandry

Without careful guidance and rigorous selection, we would still be struggling to contain half-wild gamecocks and wasting vast quantities of feed on scrawny pigs and cows. Animal husbandry is the means by which the beasts that once roamed free and fierce were tamed and "improved" for human use.

It might be tempting to look at a fat sow suckling her litter or the gallons of milk given by a cow and think that the evolution of these creatures is mostly over. This is a poor way of thinking. In reality, breeders are always striving to make healthier, more efficient animals, and they are still making progress. One need only compare the broilers of the 1950s to those of today to see it.

Always choose the biggest and the best of your livestock to breed, including the fastest growers, the most fertile, and those with mild temperaments. Good breeding can be undone in only a few generations, but significant improvements take years of careful dedication. The big hog may look delicious, but he's better saved to produce hundreds of big offspring instead.

Breeding

Some livestock are left to sort out nature on their

own, while others are kept apart until it is time to breed. Most poultry, for example, are housed together because of the prodigious, continuous output of the females. Goats, meanwhile, must be kept separate lest the buck impart his unique scent to the does' milk. Overbreeding among large animals or rabbits is also a physical health risk.

Animals, as a general rule, know how to accomplish the act of mating itself. It is up to humans to know when to bring them together, as well as how to handle them safely during the encounter. The table below should give an idea of what to expect every year from a single female:

Livestock	Offspring Per Year
Poultry – Small	Up to 200
Poultry – Large	Up to 50
Goats	Average 2
Pigs	Average 16
Sheep	Average 2
Cattle	Average 1
Rabbits	Average 40
Llamas & Alpacas	Average 1

Keeping males of any species is something of a mixed bag. They are more aggressive, tend to eat more, and are really only useful for a few minutes every year.

Because of this, many small farmers instead choose to pay a small stud fee to a local herd owner or order semen for artificial insemination. Artificial insemination is quite simple and allows for a greater genetic variety, but it sometimes results in lower fertility than a standard breeding.

Choose a male that complements your female and will give you the sort of offspring you desire. A Boer goat buck over a dairy doe produces robust and meaty kids while the mother still provides copious milk. In such a way, a single breeding produces an optimal amount of both. Always choose males with proven fertility and who appear to be in excellent health. Ask for breeding papers or to see his other children and family for a better understanding of his genetic background.

Once the deed is done, the mother is free to return to her home and wait for the big day.

Eggs

Poultry are the easiest livestock to raise, though they are more hands-on if you choose to incubate and rear the young yourself. I use chickens here as a model, but the basics apply to almost every bird.

Hens lay eggs in groups called clutches. The high-production egg layers of today have had the mothering instinct bred out of them, but when a traditional hen sees a large bunch of eggs and feels that her environment is safe, her brain may switch over into broody mode. From that point on, the hen is fixated on nothing but sitting on those eggs and ensuring that they hatch. She will occasionally get up for a quick gulp of water and some food, but for the most part she remains on the nest, turning the eggs as needed.

A good hen will brood the eggs until they hatch and then protect her chicks until they are old enough to join the larger flock. Other chickens do not have a protective nature, however, and should be kept separate from the new family. Keeping a large brooder will give the mother a safe place to protect her chicks until they are at least two months old.

Of course, the thing about birds is that they aren't very clever and they are not predictable. One day a hen will decide to brood, but by the next she may have lost interest. Some never develop the instinct at all. Others kill their chicks as soon as they hatch.

If you lack a few reliable broody hens (Cochins, Silkies, and Orpingtons are renowned mothers and worth their feed,) incubating is a surer method that can result in more chicks all at once.

An incubator controls humidity and temperature for the eggs inside it, which are vulnerable to fluctuations of either. More expensive incubators also turn the eggs automatically. You can build your own incubator, but a good, medium-sized one is only about $200.

While the eggs are developing, periodically remove them and shine a bright light into them to check their progress. The embryo inside starts as a small dark spot, then develops a spider-web of veins and slowly transforms into a peeping, pecking chick.

When the chicks begin to pip, or break the shell, do not assist them. It is tempting, especially when the chick takes hours or even days or appears to be having difficulties. Helping the chick along is kindhearted but often results in death for the chick, which has not had time to absorb the last of its yolk or is simply not strong enough to survive. Losses are common and normal, and very few people manage a perfect hatch rate.

Once the chick is out, let it remain in the incubator for at least two days. If it were hatched by its mother, it would be in a similar environment underneath her, waiting for its siblings to hatch. Losing humidity by opening the incubator damages any chicks still hatching. Eventually the chicks can be moved to a warm, dry location, usually the brooder. There's no rush to give them food or water; they can live comfortably off their absorbed yolk for at least four days.

Birthing

Mammals are more complex animals when it comes to reproduction. As a result, when something goes wrong with either the mother or the baby, you could lose one or both in one fell swoop. If you have kept rabbits, you should already have experience with birthing, but larger mammals are more risky. Seek out the help of an experienced individual or veterinarian for your first few births, and have him or her show you what can go wrong as well.

Most livestock prefer to give birth in a secluded area either late at night or very early in the morning. As the farmer charged with caring for them, this presents a challenge for you. Keep an eye on pregnant animals nearing their due date and bring them inside to a warm and sheltered pen when they begin to appear agitated or show the other tell-tale signs of an approaching birth. This includes a relaxed vulva and hind end, swollen or dripping teats, and even contractions if she is far enough along.

A good mother gives birth far more easily than we humans do. Several heaves combined with careful pulls should bring the baby out into the world when the time comes. The consequences of an abnormal birth, however, can be costly and heartbreaking. If the baby is turned wrong or suffers from some other malady, decisions must be made quickly.

Assuming everything goes well, you will have a happy, if tired, mother and a doe-eyed youngster or two eager for some milk. Watch to make sure she accepts her young before leaving them together. Orphans must be removed and bottle-fed to survive or given to a willing surrogate.

Castration

It often makes sense to keep altered males. A beef steer, for example, grows faster, develops finer meat, and is easier to manage than his intact brother. He also won't breed any females pastured with him.

There are a number of ways to castrate animals. If you are squeamish, leave it to a veterinarian. Otherwise, make sure you have the basics down before attempting it on your own. An improper castration is immensely painful for the animal and may lead to a host of health problems.

Banding is one of the most common castration methods, especially for homesteaders. It is bloodless and won't traumatize the male. Banding is done early. An applicator stretches a band tight, which is then passed over the testicles and allowed to snap around them. The scrotum withers and falls away within a few weeks with little to no pain to the livestock.

A burdizzo, or emasculator, crushes the spermatic cord, starving the testicles and causing them to with much like in banding. It is another preferable method because there is little room for error, and it does not leave an open wound.

The third method is surgical castration. The scrotum is disinfected and then sliced open to reveal the testicles, which are removed. The wound is then left to heal naturally. Obviously, this is the most difficult procedure and can lead to serious ramifications if done poorly.

Growing Feed

The gardening section for this year covered staple, nutrient-rich plants that are excellent for humans but even better for livestock. If you have the space, you can grow almost all of your animals' diets and come one step closer to real self-sufficiency. The trick is to work out seasonal recipes based on each species' nutrition requirements and develop a good estimate of how much of each plant or mineral is needed.

Plants to Feed

Grasses, grains, and soy tend to make up the bulk of livestock feed, but there are a few other plants worth knowing.

The mangel beet, for example, is an old standby of homesteaders because it is cold-tolerant and a favorite of poultry and ruminants alike. They grow to be 10 pounds or more and make for a sweet supplement. They do present a storage problem because of their size; root cellar conditions are ideal. Introduce mangels slowly to ruminants.

Also grow carrots, turnips, sunflowers, kale, chard and anything else your livestock enjoy. No home recipe is the same, because no pasture or climate is the same. What matters is that the base nutritional requirements of each animal are met without reaching critically high levels. To get started, head to a local organic feed mill and see what they are mixing into their respective feeds. They should have a reasonable grasp of the native plants and minerals and be able to advise a complete recipe. From there, tweak nutrient levels and ingredients based on your own experience with feed.

Pasture Rotation

Anyone who has kept chickens confined to a run knows what happens when animals are given insufficient room to sustain themselves. Grass and plants are quickly killed off, leaving only mud and rocks behind. New growth is snapped up immediately, meaning once a pasture or run goes to dirt it will stay that way for as long as the animals are on it.

If you are willing to supply all of your livestock's feed, there is nothing particularly inhumane about these conditions. It's better, however, to save yourself some money and maintain healthy pastures for your livestock. It gives animals something to do during the day and a natural diet that produces wonderful meat and dairy. If you question the extent of these benefits, crack open a free-ranged chicken egg next to one from the store. The yolks should be visible proof of the drastic effect diet plays on a finished product.

If you do not have acres and acres to devote to large grazing animals like goats, pigs, sheep, and cattle, pasture rotation makes grass-fed livestock possible. Think of it this way: three small pastures will provide more grass for livestock than a single pasture of the same combined size. The more pastures the better, but a three-pasture rotation system should keep most livestock in grass.

Rotating pasture is good for animals but also for the soil. Rather than breaking down top soils and root systems, the ground is given a chance to recover from the bruising of hooves and tearing teeth. Manure left behind has time to be absorbed into the soil, boosting further growth.

As a general rule, grass should be at least 6" high before animals are turned out onto a pasture, and they should be removed once the average length has been reduced to 3". This exchange rate depends on how many animals you are keeping on how much, and how lush, land. Plan to keep each pasture in rotation for four to six months, and have an additional pasture to rest each year. That means that if you are dividing pastures for four months each, then the area needs to be divided into at least four sections. Use the resting pasture to grow hay if you want to keep it productive.

Growing Pasture

Besides harvesting and storing feed, you can also give it to livestock fresh from the ground. Sowing a mixture of healthy plants creates better pasture, meaning quicker growth and more balanced nutrition. It also helps control what your animals are eating and limits the incursion of toxic or useless weeds.

Good pasture is a mix of grasses and legumes for grazing animals and rough shrubs and trees for foragers. The two styles complement each other if the land is suitable. Try planting a mix of alfalfa, oats, brome, clovers, and grasses. Go light on fattening alfalfa. Plant choice is largely determined by soil nutrients and the rainfall in your area. Amending the soil after running a nutrient test opens up your options considerably. Drought-tolerant grasses survive into even the driest summers, but they are less appealing to animals and less nutritious.

It is best to start with fresh, tilled ground to give the seeds a fighting chance against weeds. Broadcast and lightly cover the seeds, and allow them to grow normally. A good pasture develops a natural ecosystem that only needs to be refreshed every few years if not overgrazed.

Basic Veterinary Care

Animals are expensive enough when things go as planned, let alone when they go awry. Veterinary care, which is needed in some capacity for nearly all livestock, is a big cost that eats into the final "price" of all animal products. For this reason, most farmers teach themselves basic veterinary practices like giving shots, delivering, deworming, and providing light first aid.

As with many entries in this book, caring for animals is a matter of owner discretion. When in doubt, call in a professional, and don't start throwing everything at the wall to see what sticks. Part of being a responsible livestock manager is ensuring that every animal is as healthy and comfortable as possible at all times, and poor treatment just leads to a sicker creature than you started with. A good veterinarian is worth the price. Do not hesitate to call one in.

Recognizing Illness

Every species, and to an extent every breed, is different. With familiarity, however, you should have a basic idea of what a healthy animal looks like and be able to pick out problems quickly.

Some common things to watch for include: lethargy, loss of appetite, swelling, dehydration, overheating, diarrhea, constipation, visible injury, parasites, abscesses, and growths.

When something isn't right, look the animal over for visible signs of illness. Injuries and swelling are the most readily apparent. If the cause remains a mystery, bring in a veterinarian for a more thorough analysis.

Deworming

Deworming livestock is the easiest piece of veterinary care. Worms are a type of parasite that feed off of nutrients the animal ingests. In small numbers they reduce feed efficiency and overall health, but a large infestation can kill.

Send in samples to a veterinarian for a fecal examination. He or she will identify any parasites, the severity of the load, and suggest the proper treatment. Not all wormers kill all worms.

Wormers are applied in a number of ways. Some are delivered through the water supply, others are poured along the back, and still more are applied as a paste or injected into the skin. For large animals, the pour-on method is safest, whereas with chickens adding wormer to the water is the most practical option.

The most important thing is getting the dosage right. Too little builds resistance and won't solve the issue, whereas too much can damage the animal's system. Wormers are typically applied in multiple doses over a week or two. During this time and for several weeks afterward, do not consume any products from the animal.

Injections

Giving an injection is often the most frightening veterinary procedure for homesteaders, and for good reason. Like small children, animals don't like getting stuck with a needle and they have a lot more muscle when they start to squirm. A misguided jab is painful and potentially dangerous to the livestock. Shots are typically given in the neck or shoulder.

As a small farmer, your shot administration should be somewhat limited. Young animals are given vaccines to protect them from various illnesses, wormers are sometimes injectable, and you may occasionally come across a disease that requires shots.

The two main types of injection are subcutaneous and intramuscular. Subcutaneous injections are administered by pinching loose skin and squirting the fluid in the space between the folds. Intramuscular injections are firmly inserted into the muscle, taking care not to hit bones or blood vessels in the process.

The third type of injection, intravenous, is best left to a trained professional and is applied directly into the bloodstream.

Always use a clean, sterile needle and watch the animal afterward for signs of allergic reactions.

First Aid

There are also the every-day scrapes and bruises animals pick up in the process of being animals. They rub up on fence posts, fight, and manage to place themselves in the strangest situations imaginable. Even the most experienced farmer is sometimes taken aback by an animal's capacity for mischief.

Use common sense when dealing with injury. If it is bleeding profusely or becoming infected, see a vet. Otherwise, it can be tended to on the homestead with some basic first aid.

For an all-around first-aid kit, I recommend having the following on hand at all times:

- Alcohol wipes
- Antibiotic ointment
- Cotton balls
- Syringes
- Flashlight with batteries
- Gauze
- Iodine
- Latex gloves
- Pocket knife
- Probiotics and electrolytes
- Scissors
- Styptic powder or corn starch
- Tweezers
- Wire cutters

You may need to pick up other supplies for specific scenarios, but these items are meant to handle general emergencies and control the situation until more comprehensive treatment can begin.

MAKING A LIVING

Running a small farm is a part-time job by itself, and many homesteaders dream of a day when they can actually live off of their land without needing to head into the office every morning.

Earning a sustainable income off of property is not easy, and the less land you have the less likely it is to happen. However, there are plenty of ways to work from home, and if your efforts at farming have been successful you should have a much lower cost of living than other families.

If you are serious about quitting your job to work from home or would like to generate some extra spending money, you must first set a goal for yourself. That might mean calculating how much you need to survive for a year or deciding that you would like to cover the basic expenses involved with livestock and property maintenance. Whatever it is, set a number.

You may not reach it in one year or even five, but it will always be there to work toward.

For homesteaders, there are two main sources of income: the fruits of farming and a home-based business. Each has its own potential, advantages, and drawbacks, and remember that if they don't work out there's no shame in having at least one household member with a full- or part-time job to cover expenses.

Earning an Income on the Farm

Sadly, earning a living on a small farm is no longer as feasible as it once was. Increasing regulations meant to improve conditions in factory farms apply to small enterprises as well, making it now almost impossible for family operations to turn a profit. Dairying, for example, is so bogged down by rules, paperwork, and inspections that maintenance costs often outweigh the price of milk. Dairy products like cheese and yogurt are subjected to the same scrutiny. Economies of scale simply aren't in our favor.

How, then, can the small farmer make a living? The most lucrative route is to appeal to America's growing nostalgia for locally grown foods and the farm experience. Raw vegetables and fruits are the easiest foods to sell, besides perhaps eggs. Check out local co-ops and farmers' markets to learn the safety standards in your area.

Grass-fed meat is also in high demand, but it is trickier to sell and a wrong move may end in fines and confiscations. The best solution is to sell customers a share of a cow, goat, pig, or flock and have it butchered by a certified professional.

The other product selling well right now is livestock. As more and more people start to reclaim their food production, they turn to local breeders to get their herds started and supplemented. Breed the best you can and be accessible to both future and past clients to succeed here.

Finally, you can make a fair income selling the farm lifestyle to tourists and families. This includes corn mazes, hay rides, petting zoos, you-pick orchards, and bed and breakfasts. Teach classes on your farming specialties. If you are willing to put in some attractive landscaping and open your property to visitors, you may find an eager audience.

With the right dedication and a solid understanding of the law, you can try your hand at any business you please. Make soaps, sell preserves, breed the finest dairy sheep in the nation, but don't bank your entire livelihood on an unproven model. More than ever, this is a shaky time for small farms, especially commercially. We are competing with huge corporations that can beat our prices almost every time. Aim to provide for yourself and your family and cover your daily expenses. Whatever else you make is a bonus.

Working From Home

The other form of financial independence is to make a living at home through some type of business. The Internet has made it possible to live off of more than just your hands. Your mind is a valuable tool and there are a million different uses for it.

Do you have a knack for woodwork? Build and sell chicken coops and rabbit hutches, or take on even larger assignments. Become a freelance writer or graphic designer, help companies sell products through affiliate marketing, or sell your artwork to a global audience. Make an app for smartphones, or run a weekly newsletter. People are looking to buy just about everything; your job is to make them buy it from you.

There are thousands of books out there on this subject, and a few of them are even worth reading. To get started, assess your own skills. Write everything down and start doing your homework. There is no guarantee of success, but if you are truly dedicated to quitting your day job this is the way to go, and there really is no limit to income potential.

YEAR SIX AND BEYOND

MOVING FORWARD

It might be cheating for a "five-year guide" to have a year six, but pretending that the goal of self-sufficiency ends in a mere five years would be hopelessly naïve. The five-year figure is simply an optimistic projection and recommendation following a logical progression. In reality, it may take you 10 years to achieve half the items covered in this book. And that's fine!

Every step away from the modern food industry or a forgetful and meaningless culture is a positive one. Even if you are derailed by financial or personal woes, be proud of what you do achieve.

When I began writing this book, I never intended for it to reach this length. But as I continued outlining, I found more and more topics that I wanted to mention, until it grew into something larger. There's so much that farmers take for granted until we're forced to sit down and elaborate.

This is not the definitive guide to anything, but I hope it has offered you a broader perspective on what it means to be self-sufficient and how to go about realizing your own goals.

As you continue, you may find that owning a homestead is much like my experience writing this book. You will constantly discover new things you want to add. Some stay around and become new habits, while others fade away as vague disappointments. Keep an open mind and don't be afraid to try anything that catches your eye.

Finally, I'd like to close out by wishing you all the best, no matter where your life takes you. Homesteading isn't for everyone, and whether you are still part of the culture 20 years from now or living in a cramped city apartment, the fact that you have even taken an interest in breaking away from the norm is a positive sign.

Share what you know and help your community in any way you can. These are times when small individuals, faced with the greater collective, must stick together and continue to spread the idea of sustainable living one acre at a time.

Writing is, in part, how I am able to pay for life on a homestead. If you enjoyed the book, or even if you hated it, I'd appreciate your taking the time to leave an honest review wherever you purchased it. If you have any comments, questions, or corrections, I welcome all emails at aabarrows@gmail.com.

Works Cited

1. "Reduce Screen Time." *National Heart Lung and Blood Institute*. U.S. Department of Health & Human Services, 25 2012. Web. 23 Dec 2012.

2. "Fossil Fuel and Energy Use." *New York University*. New York University. Web. 23 Dec 2012.

3. Espinoza, Leo, Nathan Slaton, and Morteza Mozaffari. "Understanding the Numbers on Your Soil Test Report." U of A Division of Agriculture Cooperative Extension Service. University of Arkansas. Web. 23 Dec 2012.

4. Grubinger, Vern. "Managing Nitrogen on Organic Farms." *The University of Vermont*. University of Vermont Extension, n.d. Web. 23 Dec 2012.

5. Espinoza, Leo. "Profiling Food Consumption in America." United States Department of Agriculture. United States Department of Agriculture. Web. 23 Dec 2012.

6. Lockwood, David. "Home Tree Fruit Plan." *Agricultural Extension Service The University of Tennessee*. Agricultural Extension Service The University of Tennessee. Web. 23 Dec 2012.

7. Emery , Carla. The Encyclopedia of Country Living. 10th ed. Seattle, WA: Sasquatch Books, 1994. Print.

8. "Hazelnut, Arbor Day." Arbor Day Foundation. Arbor Day Foundation. Web. 23 Dec 2012.

9. Call, Robert, Richard Gibson, and Michael Kilby. "Pecan Production Guidelines For Small Orchards And Home Yards." Arizona Cooperative Extension. Arizona Cooperative Extension, n.d. Web. 23 Dec 2012.

10. Ruggieri, Cindy. "Growing Blueberries." Mother Earth News. Ogden Publications, n.d. Web. 23 Dec 2012.

11. "Grape." National gardening Association. National Gardening Association. Web. 23 Dec 2012.

12. MacDonald, James. "Economic Organization of U.S. Broiler Production." United States Department of Agriculture. United States Department of Agriculture, n.d. Web. 23 Dec 2012.

13. "Economic Data." *U.S. Poultry & Egg Association.* U.S. Poultry & Egg Association. Web. 23 Dec 2012.

14. Swiader, John. "Fertilizing Your Vegetable Garden." University of Illinois Extension. University of Illinois. Web. 23 Dec 2012.

15. "Dairy Goat Production." The Pennsylvania State University. The Pennsylvania State University. Web. 23 Dec 2012.

16. "The Goat Industry: Structure, Concentration, Demand and Growth." United States Department of

Agriculture. United States Department of Agriculture. Web. 23 Dec 2012.

17. "Complete Guide to Home Canning." United States Department of Agriculture. United States Department of Agriculture, n.d. Web. 23 Dec 2012.

18. Kleeger, Sarah, and Andrew Still. "A Guide to Seed Saving, SeedStewardship & Seed Sovereignty." *The Seea Ambassadors Project*. The Seed Ambassadors Project, n.d. Web. 23 Dec 2012.

19. "SoapCalc." SoapCalc. BRL Enterprises, 21 2012. Web. 23 Dec 2012.

20. *LDS Preparedness Manuai*. 2012 ed. Another Voice of Warning, 2012. eBook.

21. "Crop Production Information." *NDSU Extension Service*. North Dakota State University. Web. 23 Dec 2012.

Index

365

367

ABOUT THE AUTHOR

Amelia Barrows grew up in the heart of Washington State and later settled in Pennsylvania Dutch Country. She lives on a 24-acre farm and spends her days doing what she loves: gardening, tending livestock, cooking, and writing. Her own journey toward self-sufficiency continues to this day.

Made in the USA
San Bernardino, CA
20 November 2013